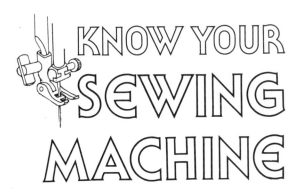

KNOW YOUR SEWING MACHINE

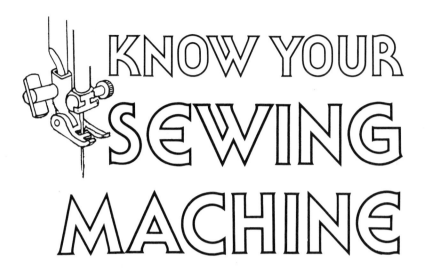

KNOW YOUR SEWING MACHINE

JACKIE DODSON

CHILTON BOOK COMPANY

RADNOR, PENNSYLVANIA

Acknowledgments

Thank You:

To the following sewing machine companies: Archer-Finesse, Bernina of America, Brother Sewing Machine Co., Elna Inc., Kenmore, Necchi Logica/Allyn International, New Home Sewing Machine Co., Pfaff American Sales Corp., Simplicity/Tacony Corp., Singer Co., Viking-White Sewing Machine Co.

To friends who answered questions when I needed help: Erick Hattenschweiler, Ed Perk, Janet Stocker, Judy Whitemyer.

A special thank you to Ed and Flo Perk, who let me work out these lessons with students at their shop.

To Caryl Rae Hancock, Nora Lou Kampe, Gail Kibiger, Pat Pasquini and Marcia Strickland for sharing ideas; Ladi Tisol who helped me before I had to ask; and Marilyn Tisol, critic, sounding-board, and special friend.

To Chuck, who took the photos and to the rest of my family, who learned to accept decorative clothing in place of mended clothing.

To Robbie Fanning, for her optimism, encouragement, and endless support.

And to my students, who kept telling me to write it all down.

Designed by William E. Lickfield
Manufactured in the United States of America

Library of Congress Cataloging in Publication Data
Dodson, Jackie.
  Know your sewing machine.
  (Creative machine arts series)
  Bibliography: p. 162
  Includes index.
  1. Machine sewing. I. Title. II. Series.
TT713.D64 1988 646.2'044 87-47978
ISBN 0-8019-7810-6 (pbk.)

1 2 3 4 5 6 7 8 9 0   7 6 5 4 3 2 1 0 9 8

Contents

Foreword

Recently I've been on an anti-clutter rampage, cleaning out closets, boxes, shelves, and files with a vengeance. I call it Playing the Game of Condominium—if I had to move to a condominium and compress all my belongings, what could I give away? The level of clutter surrounding me parallels the messy state of my brain: clean surfaces, clean mind. So I'm ruthlessly cleaning; if I haven't used it, worn it, thought of it for a year or more, out it goes.

But I cannot bring myself to throw away my bulging file of letters from Jackie Dodson, author of this book. Jackie and I met 10 years ago by accident on a tour bus in Chicago. Since then she has showered me with wacky, inspiring letters. This is a woman who is brimming with laughter and ideas, sharing both freely. Most of the letters arrived with swatches of machine-embroidered fabric pinned to them. "Have you tried this?" she'd ask, again and again.

Over the years I have learned about her machine-embroidery classes, her work with the Hinsdale Embroiderers' Guild, her ongoing family escapades. But always her letters have inspired me to run to my machine and play around with new ideas.

When it came time to revise my machine-embroidery book, I knew who to ask for help as a designer and critic: Jackie.

Now you, too, can participate in the output of this creative woman. She has developed a series of lessons that will introduce you to the full range of what you and your machine can accomplish as partners. By the end of the book, you will truly know your machine. Enjoy the trip!

Robbie Fanning

Series Editor, Creative Machine Arts, and co-author
The Complete Book of Machine Embroidery

Are you interested in a quarterly magazine about creative uses
of the sewing machine? Robbie Fanning and Jackie Dodson
are planning to start one. For more information, write:

The Creative Machine
PO Box 2634, Ste. 2
Menlo Park, CA 94026

Preface

When our children were small, we took long car trips. I remember one that took longer than planned. We all grumbled about being lost, but one of our boys said, "It's just one of Dad's long-cuts."

We loved that new word, so we came up with dictionary meanings.

Long-cut (noun): When it takes longer, but Dad convinces everyone he wanted it that way. A "little something extra." An adventure. An educational side-trip. You are happier when you finally reach your destination. And so on.

What does this have to do with the sewing machine? This book contains long-cuts, those adventurous techniques that help you and your sewing machine create something special, something out of the ordinary.

Most of us learned basic techniques of sewing when we bought our machines— how to thread it, wind a bobbin, make a buttonhole, sew a straight seam. We were shown each presser foot and how to use it. . . and, I'll bet, except for the zipper and buttonhole feet, you haven't looked at those other feet again.

But there's so much more to learn. Join me on an educational side-trip. By the time you're done with this book, you'll truly know your machine.

Let's begin by exploring how we can change a piece of fabric: we can add texture to it, appliqué it, quilt it, stitch across holes in it, draw thread out of it, gather it up and decorate it. We can stitch in space with our sewing machines, make cording–but, more importantly, once we understand the machine, it makes all our stitching easier.

As we explore all these effects, which are presented in 39 lessons, we'll make small samples for a notebook; make finished 6" squares to fit on a totebag, displaying what we've learned; and make 23 other projects. In the process of stitching the samples and projects in the book, you'll take an educational side-trip as well. You'll learn to adjust and manipulate your sewing machine until you can use it to its full potential.

This workbook of ideas does not take the place of your basic manuals. Instead, it is to be used as a reinforcement and supplement to what you already know. By working through the lessons, you will come to know your machine better.

Yes, there is much more to sewing than straight stitching. And wouldn't you rather go that long-cut route–to make your stitching more interesting and original?

In my classes I often hear this progression: "I can't do that" to "Can I really do that?" to "I can do that!" I hope this book is the next best thing to having me prompting, prodding, patting you on the back in person.

Jackie Dodson
LaGrange Park, Illinois

CHAPTER 1

Getting Started

This book is organized by the changes you can make to a piece of fabric—add stitches, add texture, subtract threads, and so on. Following this introductory chapter, each chapter consists of several lessons, and some projects. Each lesson asks you to stitch up practice samples for a notebook or for finished projects. The largest project in the book is the tote bag (directions for making it are in Chapter 12). It was designed to show off interchangeable decorative squares, which you'll make as you proceed through the lessons.

For the practice samples, you will want to set up a three-ring notebook—the kind with the largest rings—to keep track of your stitching (Fig. 1.1). Buy plastic pockets and blank notebook paper (both available at office supply stores). Write the settings you've used directly on the stitched samples and slip them into the plastic pockets for future reference.

Clip pictures from magazines that trigger ideas. Ask yourself: Could I get that effect if I loosened the bobbin? Which presser foot would I use for that? Which thread

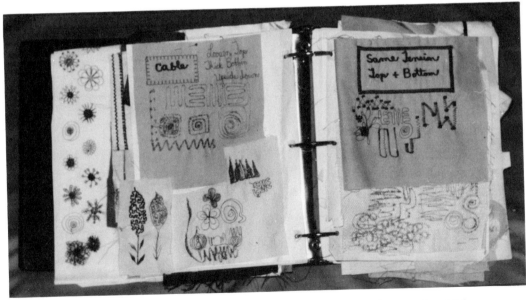

Fig. 1.1 A reference notebook, open to a page of stitch samples. Notations on the stitchery will help you reset the machine.

1

would produce loops like that? Write notes to yourself with ideas to try and add these to the notebook along with the magazine pictures.

Love your sewing machine

When I first learned to use a sewing machine, I didn't enjoy sewing the apron or quilted potholder we were required to finish for the next semester's cooking class. Not until years later when I constructed clothing that fit, gifts that were creative, upholstery that was a challenge, did I have fun with my machine. I think that you'll have fun, too, once you understand all the wonderful things you can do with your sewing machine.

I bought my first sewing machine with never a thought that the blind hem stitch could be used for more than putting in a blind hem. I'd expected to use my machine for clothing construction and repair, so it didn't occur to me that many of the built-in stitches I was using for sewing could also be used decoratively, and I could sew freely, with feed dogs lowered, to create laces, embroidery and much, much more. However, once I discovered books on machining, I began to see the sewing machine in an entirely new way: I had found a type of stitchery that suited the way I worked and had the look I loved. I've concentrated on learning everything I can about machine stitchery ever since. Notice that I did not say "machine embroidery." Embroidery is only one part of machine stitchery, which also includes making lace, needleweaving, appliquéing in creative ways, to name a few we'll touch on in this book.

If you use your machine for clothing construction, consider the possibilities of binding a pocket with your own decorated bias, hemstitching a baby bonnet, topstitching to make a seam lie flat, embroidering the edge of a placket. This book will show you the best, fastest, way of accomplishing all that.

I'm assuming you attended basic lessons when you bought your machine or, if you purchased your machine at a garage sale, that you have read and worked through the basic manual. If not, do this first. But even if you've taken the basic lessons and memorized the manual, that is just the jumping-off-place. There is so much more. A blind hem is taught in the manual, but did you know you can use it to attach elastic cord to the edge of a garment for button loops, couch down yarns and cords, attach appliqués and patch pockets? That is the type of information I've included in this book.

Let's begin by talking about your machine. First, be sure that it is in good working order: cleaned, oiled, and tuned up. I've taught long enough to know that even then, some machines have limitations. Your machine may not want to sew across an open area, mitering corners may be practically impossible, adjusting the bobbin tension may be difficult and so on. Those are problems you can get around. But there is little you can do about a machine when you've tried everything and still the bobbin jams, the satin stitch is uneven, and skipped stitches are common. If your machine gives you a headache instead of happiness, you definitely need a new machine. We may all choose our machines for different reasons, but we can agree that dependability is the most important.

When I chose my first machine, I looked for one that would accept the thickest and most tightly woven fabric made, while at the same time sewing sheers or stitching over open spaces without balking. I found one that can do all of that without changing the tension setting. However, when I want to change tensions for different effects, it's easy to change both top and bobbin and get them back to normal. And while I'm working, I can change the bobbin without taking the fabric off the bed of the machine. I didn't look for a machine that had built-in animal motifs, but I did want a built-in blind hem, an overlock stitch, and a stretch stitch. The most important automatic stitch, the zigzag, had to produce a perfect satin stitch with even edges and no skipped stitches. I got everything I wanted in my machine and it is so dependable I have to remind myself to take it in for its yearly checkup.

Today I have six machines. Each has its own personality and each is special to me. I love the perfect satin stitch on one, the feather stitch on another, the alphabet and numbers on another. Until someone custom-makes a machine to my specifications, I'm holding onto all of them.

How can you find a machine you'll love? A good starting place is to ask friends about their machines. Then check out the machines they recommend by asking for demonstrations at the dealers. Bring along fabric of every description and try them all yourself. When you finally purchase your machine, be sure you've bought only as much machine as you need — you may never use animal motifs either. The most important thing to remember is to buy one you can depend on.

So let's begin. Get out the dusty box of attachments and presser feet that came with your machine, as well as the basic manual of instructions. If you can't find the manual, contact the dealer and arrange to purchase another.

What kind of machine do you have? Not the name of it, but what are its capabilities? Can it zigzag and blind-hem stitch? Then you can stitch up the projects and complete the lessons in this book. If your machine includes other built-in stitches, you'll find they're not neglected here either.

But built-in stitches are only part of this book. Presser feet are also a part of it — an important part. When you purchased your machine, you probably asked what built-in stitches were included, but didn't think of asking about the presser feet. Most sewers don't look beyond the zigzag and zipper feet, even though presser feet expand the capabilities of the machine.

First you should know what type of presser foot fits your machine: high shank, low shank, slant shank. If the shank measures about ½″ (12 mm) from the center of the screw that holds on the presser foot to the bottom of the foot when the presser foot is down, you have a low shank machine. If the measurement is about 1″ (25 mm), your machine is high shank.

Don't be limited by using only the five or ten different presser feet that came with your machine. Once you know the type of shank your machine has, check for other feet available that weren't included when you purchased it. Also, presser feet and accessories from other machines of the same type may fit yours. Adaptor shanks are available for some to make a low shank foot fit on a high shank machine. Attachments called *ankles* allow you to use a clip-on foot for the screw-on presser foot. Check the Sources of Supply at the end of the book for mail-order catalogues where you can purchase generic presser feet — available for almost every machine. I've also discovered that sewing machine repairmen and some mail-order houses will modify presser feet to fit your machine if you can't find exactly what you need.

After looking at the presser feet you own, do you know how they are used? Turn each over and look at the bottom; it's the most important part. If it's a buttonhole foot, it will have two deep grooves to keep the fabric moving freely and in line as the beads of satin stitches are stitched in. The embroidery foot will have a wide groove cut out and sometimes it will be flared in front to allow the fabric not only to feed more freely as the decorative stitches are sewn in place, but also let corners be turned easily. There are presser feet that create pintucks, sew down braids accurately, make blind hemming a breeze, keep edges from tunneling when overcasting them, help you edge stitch or topstitch accurately and quickly—the list goes on. Find out about the ones you own and do a sample for each, write on the fabric which foot you've used, and file it in your notebook. Though I'll include some of the basics in this book, you'll learn new ways to use them as well. You can't use your machine to its full potential until you understand what the presser feet can do and then take advantage of that knowledge.

New presser feet are introduced often. Use Chart 1.1 to keep a record of the ones you have. When you come to know your sewing machine well, you will quickly realize that a jeans foot is not only for jeans, a braiding foot is not only for soutache, and many feet can do the same job.

I love all of my sewing machines! One of the reasons my enthusiasm never wanes is because I have a group of friends who also love their machines. We exchange sewing advice, pass on our creative discoveries, recommend books to each other, and sometimes meet to try new ideas. If you don't have such friends already, you'll find them in classes at your dealer, where new ideas are taught regularly.

While at the store, check out the books and magazines there. There also may be an advanced manual and leaflets about your machine, published by the sewing machine company.

What else can you use to make your sewing easier? Following is a list and description of accessories that are available.

Accessories

Bias binder

There are several types of bias binder attachments. I have one that is low-shank (it fits on my Elna and, with an adaptor shank, on my Bernina). The zigzag stitch cannot be used with all bias binders. Look for one that can, as this will enable you to attach bias with decorative stitches.

This attachment works best on straight edges and attaches binding in one operation, instead of the usual two steps.

Circle maker

Your machine may include a circle maker, which you either attach to the bed of the machine or to the presser foot.

If you don't have one, you can make your own by using transparent tape, a thumb tack and a hoop. Determine the radius of the circle you wish to stitch. Measure that distance from the needle to a place at the left of it on the machine bed. Place a tack there, point up. Hold the tack in place by pushing the tape over the point and sticking it onto the machine.

Then stretch your fabric into the hoop and place the center of the circle over the tack. Push a small cork or eraser over the point. When you rotate the hoop and stitch, you'll create a perfect circle.

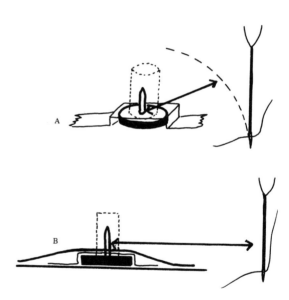

Fig. 1.2 A. Make your own circle maker by taping a thumbtack upside-down on the bed of the machine a radius away from the needle. Tape it in place. B. Place material in a hoop and stick the fabric onto the thumbtack wherever you want the center of the circle to be. Secure the fabric with a cork. Keep the fabric taut between the thumbtack and the needle as you sew a circular design.

Chart 1.1
Presser Feet Included with Machines

I've shown the presser feet included with each machine when purchased. Although some feet have letter designations (A, B, C, etc.) I've given names that explain their functions. Many more presser feet are available for all the machines—ask your dealer for a complete list. It would be impossible to list every machine, so if your machine is not listed here, use the blank column to check off which feet you own. Add the names of other feet as you purchase them to give you a complete record. Note that some brands have "2-feet-in-1"; e.g., Bernina's *cording foot* and *embroidery foot* are the same foot, but both types are checked below.

	Bernina	Brother	Elna	Kenmore	Logica Necchi	New Home	Pfaff	Simplicity	Singer	Viking	My Machine
Adaptor shank	x										
Blind stitch	x	x	x	x	x	x	x	x	x	x	
Button sew on		x		x	x		na	x	x	na	
Buttonhole	x	x	x	x	x	x	x	x	x	x	
Circle maker					x						
Cording	x					x					
Craft						x					
Darning	x	x	x		na	x	x			na	
Edging							x				
Embroidery	x	x	x	x	x	x	x		x	x	
Even feed							na	x	x		
Hemmer					x	x	x				
Jeans	x										
Monogramming		x									
Overedge	x	x			x	x	x	x		x	
Raised seam										x	
Roller			x								
Side cutter		x						x			
Special purpose	x	x			x		x	x	x	x	
Straight stitch		x		x	x			x	x		
Tailor tack	x										
Zigzag general purpose	x	x	x	x	x	x	x	x	x	x	
Zipper	x	x	x	x	x	x	x	x	x	x	

Side cutter

This accessory is like a serger, but not as fast. It cuts, sews, and neatens edges of fabric in a single operation. Use it for stay-stitching, overcasting raw edges, for French seams, and to replace ribbed bands on sweaters or T-shirts. Sew on lace edging with it, and roll and whip edges of fabrics. Topstitch using the guide at the side of the presser foot. If your machine does not have one, there is a generic accessory available (see Sources of Supply).

Eyelet maker

The Bernina eyelet maker is a collection of two awls, needle plates, and a screwdriver. Other machines include eyelets as a decorative built-in stitch or use snap-on plates that fit over the feed dogs. It's possible to buy plates with different-sized prongs, depending upon how large or small the eyelet.

There is also the Japanese flower-maker that fits on many machines and makes eyelets, as well as flower petals around the eyelet if you wish. Also, the buttonhole attachment that contains different-sized templates can be used. An eyelet template is included.

Ruffler

This attachment ruffles fabric and also pleats it. The ruffler is adjustable and you determine how full you want your ruffle or pleats to be. Always do a sample first, using the fabric you plan to use on your finished project so you can determine how much fabric you will need. The ruffles, or pleats, are not adjustable once they are sewn in.

Walking foot

The walking foot—also referred to as an even-feed attachment—may be one of your machine's accessories. If not, there are generics available. If it's necessary to have one of them adapted to your particular machine, it is worth the added expense, be-cause you will use it to stitch stripes and plaids together perfectly, to stitch plastics, leathers, knits, napped fabrics, slippery fabrics, thick fabrics, and layers of fabrics, such as quilts.

Needle plates

Needle plates other than the zigzag plate that comes with your machine are available. Each is used for a specific function. One that I own and find valuable is the straight-stitch plate. It is very helpful when I want added support around the needle hole so the fabric will not be shoved down under the plate when quilting or sewing fine, filmy fabrics. It's not necessary, but I use the straight-stitch presser foot with it for added support when I use the stitch plate.

Supplies

In addition to your sewing machine and a good supply of threads, here's a shopping list of what you'll need for the lessons. (Each lesson will give you a detailed materials list). You probably have many of the supplies in your sewing room.

1. Scissors and shears: sharp embroidery scissors, plus shears for cutting fabric and paper-cutting scissors
2. Water-erasable markers for light fabrics; white opaque permanent marker for water-soluble stabilizer; slivers of soap or light-colored chalk pencils for dark fabrics
3. T square or 6″ × 24″ (15.0cm × 61.0cm) plastic ruler; 6″ (15.0cm) and 12″ (30.5cm) see-through rulers are also helpful
4. Wood and spring-type hoops in varied sizes, maximum 7″ (17.8cm) for ease
5. Rotary cutting wheel
6. Extra bobbin case (optional)

Have fabric ready for stitching samples. A handy size is a 9″ (22.9cm) square. It will fit in the 7″ (17.8cm) hoop and can be trimmed slightly for your notebook. Cut up a variety of fabrics from extra-light-weight types like organdy, lightweights like calicos, medium-weight poplins, and heavy-weight denim. Extra-heavy-weight canvas scraps will be left over from your tote bag and can be used for experiments.

In the projects, you'll also use felt, transparent fabrics, bridal veil, ⅛″ (3.2mm) and ½″ (12.7mm) satin double-faced ribbon, lace insertion, scalloped lace, lace beading, Battenberg tape, fleece, batting, stabilizers and fusibles. Now let's discuss your choices of threads needles, and other supplies.

Threads

One of the most useful charts I have in my notebook is a piece of doubled fabric with line after line of satin stitches on it. Each row is stitched using a different type of thread. I recommend that you make one, too. More important than telling you which thread to use, your chart will graphically convince you that what is called machine-embroidery cotton is usually more lustrous and covers an area more quickly and more beautifully than regular sewing thread. It's easy to compare differences among threads.

Generally, sewing threads are not used for machine embroidery. Ordinary sewing threads are usually thicker, stretch more (if polyester), and do not cover as well as machine embroidery threads. However, for durability or when you need a certain color, try using a high quality sewing thread. I never use thread from the sale bin—the ones that are three spools for 88 cents. This thread does not hold up to heavy use; it breaks, shrinks, knots, and, after all the time spent stitching with it, looks sloppy. If I am going to take the time to sew or embroider anything, then it deserves quality thread.

Machine embroidery rayons and cottons are more lustrous and have a softer twist than ordinary sewing thread. Rayon embroidery threads are silky and loosely twisted, but if you use a #90 needle and sew evenly and at a moderate speed, they are easy to use. However, don't use rayons or any other machine embroidery threads for clothing construction because they aren't strong enough.

Besides regular sewing threads and those used for machine embroidery, there are others to become acquainted with. The fine nylon used for lingerie and woolly overlock used for serging are just a couple of them. Another is darning thread: It's often used on the bobbin for machine embroidery because it's lightweight and you can get so much more of it wound on. It comes in only a few colors, so it cannot always be used should you want the bobbin thread to be seen on the surface.

Monofilament, another popular thread, comes in two shades. One blends into light-colored fabrics, the other darks. It is not the wild, fish-line type anymore, so don't be afraid of making it work. I use it on the top and bobbin constantly.

If you use silk and silk buttonhole twists as well as fine pearl cottons, crochet and cordonnet, the needle must be large enough to keep the threads from fraying against the fabric and the eye large enough to enable the thread to go through smoothly. Sometimes top-stitching needles are called for. Or you may have to use a needle larger than you normally would embroider with.

Waxed or glacé finished quilting thread should never be used on your machine, as the finish wears off and does your machine no good.

Chart 1.2 is a handy guide, showing which needles and threads to use with which fabrics. More about where to purchase threads can be found in Sources of Supplies at the end of the book.

Needles

It is important to choose the right needle for the job. Match fabric weight, thread, and needle size, as well as type of material.

Chart 1.2
Needle and Thread Chart

Fabric	Thread	Needles
Very heavy (upholstery, canvas, denim)	Heavy-duty cotton; polyester; buttonhole twist; cordonnet	18 (110)
Heavy (sailcloth, heavy coating)	Heavy-duty cotton; polyester	16 (100)
Medium weight (wool, poplin, velvet)	Ordinary sewing cotton and polyester; machine-embroidery cotton and rayon	11, 14 (80, 90)
Lightweight (shirt cotton, dress fabrics, silk)	Extra-fine to ordinary sewing cotton and polyester	9, 11 (70, 80)
Very lightweight (lace, net, organdy, batiste)	Extra-fine sewing cotton and polyester	8, 9 (60, 70)

The lighter the material, the smaller the needle and finer the thread should be. The heavier the fabric, the larger the needle should be.

Like presser feet, needles come in different sizes and shapes and produce different effects. I once had a student in quilting class who struggled to get a needle out of her machine—it was rusted in. "I don't do much sewing," she said. (Why didn't that surprise me?) No matter how mind-boggling this sounds, I know that few sewers change needles unless they break, even though a new needle keeps thread from fraying, fabric from being damaged, and your stitches from skipping. The correct size and shape enables you to stitch through the heaviest or the flimsiest materials with ease. Also, hemstitching and double needles allow you to create unique, decorative work.

But all needles do not fit all machines. Check your manual to find out which needle system to buy for yours.

Needles are available in pierce point, used for woven fabrics; and ball point, used for knits to minimize cutting threads and causing runs in the fabric. The universal-point needle is all-purpose and can be used

	Very Fine	Fine	Med.	Strong	Large	Very Large
U.S.	—	9	11/12	14	16	18
Europe.	60	70	80	90	100	110

for knits, as well as woven fabrics. Instead of cutting through the fabric, the slightly rounded point deflects off the threads and slips between them. Because of its versatility, it is the needle in greatest use today.

Following is a list of needles and their uses:

Universal Needles: All-purpose sewing.
Fine Ballpoint Needles: Fine fabrics, including knits and wovens.
Medium Ballpoint Needles: Heavier knitted fabrics.
Medium Ballpoint Stretch Needles: Special needles for problem stretch fabrics.
Extra-Fine Point Needles: Used to pierce closely woven fabrics such as canvas or denim; often called jeans needles.
Topstitching Needles: Equipped with an eye and thread groove larger than a

regular needle of the same size. Use buttonhole twist or double thread when topstitching. Use them for embroidery, too.

Magic Needles: Identified by their black top and the two eyes. They're used for basting with the 730 and 830 Berninas. The lower eye can be threaded for regular sewing. If you plan to use it for basting, thread the top eye.

Double and Triple Needles: Used for sewing with more than one thread on top. Double needles come in four sizes—which designate the width between needles—1.6mm, 1.8mm, 2mm, 4mm.

Hemstitching Needles: Double and single types.

Leather Needles: Often called wedge needles because of their cutting points. Use them on real suede and leather. Or use a regular #110 needle in place of a leather needle.

To keep your machine running trouble-free, change the needle often. Be sure the needle is straight and has no burr on the point. Damaged needles damage fabric and machines.

If your machine is noisy and is skipping stitches, change the needle (assuming the machine is oiled and clean). Be sure you've used the correct needle system for your machine and be certain you've placed the needle in the machine correctly. Most of the time a damaged needle is the only problem—and an easy one to rectify.

To make it easier for you to prepare appropriate supplies before beginning the lessons, let's discuss items often called for and the terms I'll use.

Batting, fleece, and fiberfill

Batting, both cotton and polyester, is used between fabric layers for quilting. Different weights and sizes are available, as well as different qualities. For our use, most of the projects can be quilted with bonded batting, which holds together firmly, or with fleece, which is a filler that's thinner than bonded batting and about as thick as a heavy wool blanket. Alternative fillers can be flannel, when only a light garment is desired, or a wool blanket. Fiberfill is the shredded batting used to fill toys. Or stuff toys with batting.

Fusibles

Fusibles are used to hold appliqués to background fabrics so edges are held firmly for the final step of stitching them in place. Plastic sandwich bags or cleaner's garment bags can be used. Stitch Witchery, Fine Fuse, Magic Polyweb and Jiffy Fuse are commercial fusible webbings. To use, place them between two pieces of fabric and press with a hot iron until the webbing melts and holds the two fabrics together. Use a Teflon pressing sheet to protect your iron and also to allow you to press the fusible to one fabric at a time. The Applique Pressing Sheet or Teflon sheet has eliminated any problem with the fusible melting on your iron: it looks like opaque wax paper, is reusable, and comes in handy sizes.

A fusible webbing already backed by paper, which saves one step in application, is called Wonder-Under Transfer Fusing Web. Draw your design directly onto the paper and place it over the appliqué fabric. Press for a few seconds, which fuses the webbing to the fabric. Then cut out the pattern and pull the paper away from the webbing. Place the appliqué on the background fabric. Cover with a damp cloth and press (wool setting) for 10 seconds. Stitch in place.

Appliqué papers are paper-backed products that look very much like freezer wrap, but act like the transfer web. One side of the paper has a glue finish.

See Chapter 4 for more about fusibles.

Stabilizers

Stabilizers are used behind fabric to keep it from puckering when you embroider. At one time, we used typing paper, but today we have more choices of stabilizers, available at fabric and quilt shops and through mail-order (see Sources of Supplies).

The old standby, typing paper, still does the job. Or, use shelf paper when stitching large pictures and adding-machine tape for long strips of embroidery. A problem with paper is that it dulls machine needles faster than tear-away stabilizers do. It's also harder to remove from the back of the embroidery, although dampening the paper will help.

Another stabilizer you probably have in the cupboard is plastic-coated freezer wrap. I find I'm using it more and more. If I'm embroidering a fabric that could be damaged by the hoop, I back it instead with freezer wrap, which I iron to the back of the fabric. The freezer paper adheres to the fabric and stiffens it. When I finish my embroidery, I peel off the freezer paper. I like using it if I have a small piece of fabric to embroider. I iron the small piece to a larger, easier-to-manipulate piece of freezer paper.

Tear-away stabilizers come in crisp or soft finishes and some are iron-ons. When embroidering, place them between the fabric and machine. When the embroidery is completed, they tear away from the fabric easily.

Don't confuse stabilizers with interfacings. Interfacings are permanent and don't tear away. They can be used, of course, and so can fabrics like organdy, but they are usually used when you plan to leave the stabilizer on the back of the embroidery after it's completed.

One of the newest stabilizers is a thin film of plastic, available by the sheet or the yard, that will dissolve when wet. Clamp it into the hoop along with the fabric. It is transparent, and can be used on top of the embroidery, too. It can be marked on, but choose a water-erasable marker or permanent white opaque marker that will not leave ink on your embroidery when the plastic is dissolved. When your embroidery is completed, rinse out the stabilizer. It will become gooey, then disappear. I'll refer to it as water-soluble stabilizer.

Helpful hints for sewing

Before beginning to sew, check out the following general helpful hints:

1. Every machine has its own idiosyncracies, so the settings I recommend for each lesson are only suggestions; your machine may prefer different ones.

2. Take your sewing machine in for regular check-ups whether you think it needs it or not. Between checkups, keep it clean and oil it if it is not self-lubricating. It should be oiled after every 10 or 12 hours of use. Or, if your machine starts clacking instead of humming, get out the oil can, but take it easy. There are more problems with over-oiling than with too little. To be sure the oil works its way through the areas that need lubricating, oil *before* sewing rather than when your sewing is completed. Check your manuals to learn all the spots on your machine that need oil.

3. No matter what machine you have, you must keep the inside free of lint and threads. Clean the bobbin area by first removing the bobbin, then wiping out all the lint. A Q-tip works well and so does canned air. It's used for cameras and is wonderful to blow out lint from hard-to-reach areas. I sometimes vacuum out lint from inside the machine. Remember to clean the feed dogs whenever you finish sewing or during a long period of stitching nappy fabrics such as corduroy, fur, or velvets. Always clean during and after using a side-cutter accessory.

After the inside has been freed of lint, put a drop of oil in every spot that needs lubricating.

Now gather your supplies together and begin the adventure—to know your sewing machine.

CHAPTER 2

Adding Stitches to Your Fabric

- ■ Lesson 1. Using built-in stitches
- ■ Lesson 2. Using free machining

In this chapter you'll become acquainted with the range of stitches your machine can produce. By the end of it, you'll easily switch back and forth from stitching with the feed dogs up to stitching with feed dogs down or covered. To demonstrate your new facility, you'll make beautiful small buttons and pendants.

Lesson 1. Using built-in stitches

The first thing I did when I bought my machine was to try all the built-in stitches. I wanted a reference, so I sewed stitches in rows at different widths and lengths and put them in a notebook, along with notations from the Basic Manual. I was determined to know my sewing machine, and this has been so helpful to me that I've made it your first lesson too.

To save you time, practical and decorative stitches have been built into sewing machines: I classify them as "closed" and "open." "Closed" refers to those where the beauty is in stitching it close together (wide stitch width, stitch length almost 0 to 1/2), like the satin stitch or scallop stitch. "Open" built-in stitches, like the serpentine stitch, blind hem, vari-overlock and gathering stitch, are usually sewn at a stitch length longer than 1/2.

To practice the built-in stitches and make a record of them, first set up your machine as indicated in the box at the beginning of the lesson.

Stitch lines of the built-in stitches found on your machine (Fig. 2.1). The striped fabric will help you keep them straight.

Stitch width: varies
Stitch length: varies
Needle position: center
Needle: #90/14
Feed dogs: up
Presser foot: open embroidery foot
Tension: *top,* normal; *bobbin,* normal
Fabric suggestion: medium-weight striped cotton
Thread: machine-embroidery to contrast with fabric, different colors in top and bobbin
Accessories: fine-point marker
Stabilizer: tear-away or freezer paper

Start by using the settings suggested in the manual. Vary the settings as you stitch, making the stitches wider and narrower, longer and shorter. If there is a setting you find particularly useful, mark it right on the fabric with a marker to show where that setting begins.

This is a good time to determine the precise width and length settings for the best-looking closed, decorative stitches.

Using different colors of thread on top

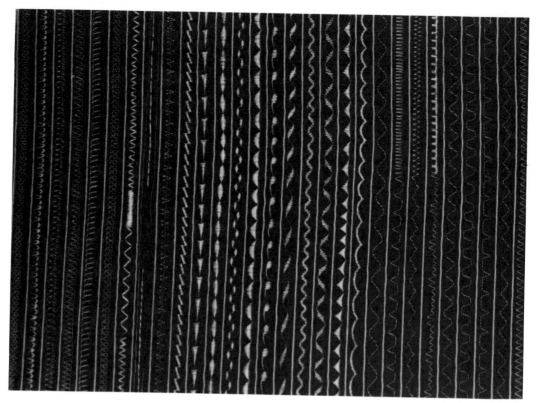

Fig. 2.1 Striped fabric is used to make a record of all the built-in stitches on my Bernina 930.

and bobbin will help you adjust the machine to find the perfect stitch. Adjust tension by loosening the top tension slightly and leaving the bobbin tension normal. The top thread should be pulled down and show underneath the fabric and should mound slightly on top when making satin stitches.

Start by stitching the zigzag, with the widest stitch width, stitch length 2. Adjust the length as you stitch until the satin stitch is perfect. This will be somewhere between 0 and 1/2 length. Write the setting on the sample.

When you finish your record of the built-in stitches, practice mirror images. This is

as simple as pushing a button on some machines. If you have one without this capability, now is the time to practice and learn to make them. Check your manual.

There are a number of variables with mirror images. Are you feeding the fabric through exactly? Don't pull on one side when the other has been fed through freely. Did you start the second row at exactly the right spot? Just one stitch off will make a difference. Do you have the same thickness of fabric under both sides of the design? If you're stitching on top of a seam allowance, the needle may go off the two layers.

Not only can you make a mirror image

by pushing a button or dialing the change on some machines, but you can also program the machine to stop after the last stitch of the design. Also, on some machines, the design can be elongated, narrowed and balanced. Make a record of each possibility if you have this kind of machine.

As you sew line after line of practical and decorative stitches, imagine how they can be used. For example, the blind-hem stitch is used for blind hems and for the tricot scalloped hem. But it can also be an invisible way of stitching on a patch pocket or an appliqué, or the stitch to use when couching down heavy cords.

Lesson 2. Using free-machining: darning, whipping, feather stitching

In free machining, you—not the presser foot—control the movement of the fabric, which in turn determines the length of the stitch. With fabric stretched tightly in a hoop, it is easy to move your work forward, backward, in circles, whatever way you wish.

I suggest working with a wooden hoop

Stitch width: varies
Stitch length: 0
Needle position: center
Needle: #80 and double needle
Feed dogs: lowered or covered
Presser foot: darning foot or none
Tension: *top*, slightly loosened; *bobbin*, normal
Fabric: light-colored, medium-weight fabric, such as poplin—scrap for practice; 18" x 18" (45.7cm x 45.7cm) square for your notebook
Thread: one color for top, another for bobbin; both should contrast with fabric
Accessories: wrapped wooden hoop no larger than 7" (17.8cm), fine-point marker
Stabilizer: tear-away or freezer paper

when first learning machine stitchery. Choose one that has a smooth finish, and slips easily under the darning foot. But whatever wooden hoop you use, be sure it is the screw type, as that will hold the fabric tightly. To be sure that it does, the inside ring of the wooden hoop should be wound with narrow twill tape. This keeps

Fig. 2.2 Free-machine darning stitches were used to make a picture.

the fabric from slipping. Take a few hand stitches at the end of the tape to hold it firmly.

If your needle will not clear the hoop you've chosen, turn the hoop on its side and slip it under the darning foot or put the hoop together and carve out a small wedge to make it easier. Then wrap the inside part with tape.

Fabric is placed in the hoop upside-down from the way you would put it in a hoop for hand embroidery (Fig. 2.3). Pull the cloth as tightly as you can. Tighten the screw; pull again; tighten. Tap on the fabric. If it sounds like a drum, it is tight enough. You may or may not want to use a stabilizer under a hoop, depending upon the effect you want and the weight of the fabric.

You can stitch with a darning foot on or without a presser foot (but keep your fingers a safe distance from the needle!).

It is possible to stitch freely without a hoop if you use your fingers to hold the fabric taut while stitching. If you don't use a hoop—or if you use a spring-type hoop—use a darning foot to prevent skipped stitches. It will hold the fabric down each time the machine makes a stitch so the

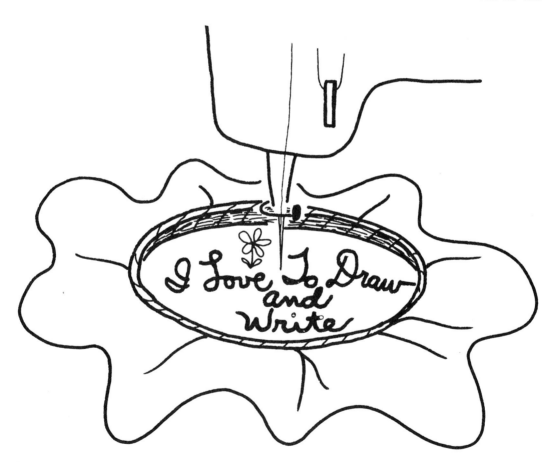

Fig. 2.3 Tighten fabric in a hoop. The fabric rests against the bed of the machine, with the material topside up for machine embroidery.

14

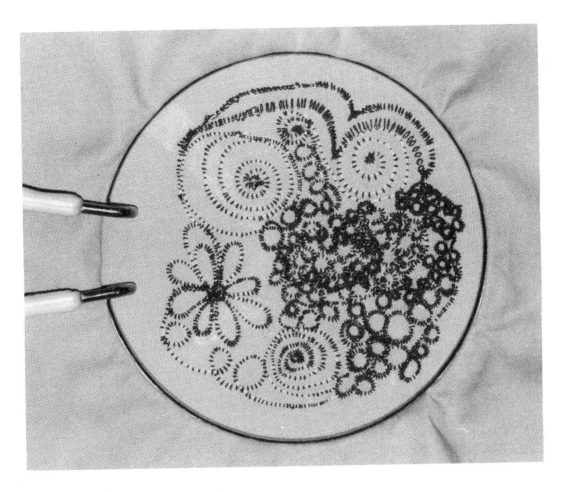

Fig. 2.4 Whipping and feather stitching.

threads interlock correctly underneath. Also, use a stabilizer under the fabric to keep the stitches from puckering.

The two samples in this lesson will give you practice in control and coordination. One sample will be for practice; the other, for your notebook. Keep a record of the new-found stitches you create with your machine and your imagination.

Free machining—darning, whipping and feather stitching—takes practice, but it is worth every minute. It opens up a new world of stitchery to you.

First, you are going to learn to draw, write, and sketch with your machine. It's called the darning stitch.

Set up your machine for darning. Always begin by dipping the needle into the fabric and bringing the bobbin thread to the top. Hold both threads to the side while stitching in one place several stitches to anchor the thread. Clip off the ends. When you begin your stitchery, start slowly. Practice moving the hoop slowly, as well. You must coordinate the speed at which you move your hoop and your sewing speed. It is not necessary to stitch at top speed—moderate speed is fine. You'll soon

Fig. 2.5 Draw 36 squares on a piece of fabric, then fill them in with the new stitches and techniques you've learned and will learn. Be sure to record machine settings.

learn how fast is right for you and for the particular stitching you are creating.

Move the hoop back and forth, then in circles—remember the old Palmer Method exercises for handwriting? Stitch faster; move your hoop faster. Then write your name, draw a picture of a tree, your dog, an old flame. It doesn't matter how well you draw; you are really practicing control.

Change to zigzag and try it all over again. Yes, it will take awhile to gain absolute control, but don't give up. Stitch tiny fill-in spirals, figure eights and jigsaw patterns.

Now stitch, hesitate, stitch. The bobbin color may come to the top. Good! That's what we want. To make sure it does, tighten the top tension slowly. When you see the bobbin thread, note where the tension dial is set and write this on the sample. This type of stitchery is called whipping. If the hoop is moved slowly and the machine run very fast, a nubby, thickened line of bobbin thread will appear on the surface. It can be used in place of the darning stitch when embroidering—or used with it for variety. Whipping can be seen in the tiny circles of dark bobbin thread in Fig. 2.4.

With the top tension very tight and the bobbin tension loosened, stitch straight lines, circles and spirals. Move the hoop quickly. The top thread is visible as a straight line on top of the fabric. Covering it are looping, feathery bobbin stitches. This is an exaggeration of whipping, which is called feather stitching. This can be seen in the hoop in some of the small circles as I went from tight to tighter top tension, and in the larger, spiky spirals (Fig. 2.4) that occurred when I loosened the bobbin tension until there was no resistance on the thread.

Practice is the only way to learn control. When you feel you have accomplished coordination between moving the hoop and the speed of the machine, make the following record of what you've learned: On the 18″ x 18″ (45.7cm x 45.7cm) square of fabric, draw a grid of 3″ (7.6cm) squares, six across, six down (Fig. 2.5). Then fill in your squares with examples of free machining—darning, whipping and feather stitching. Use both straight stitches and zigzag stitches in your squares. Try built-in stitches, too. You can stitch your own designs or use mine. But as you practice, write the machine settings on the fabric. Slip this into your notebook. Add new stitches as you discover them and refer to your notebook regularly for stitches you want to use on a project.

For variety, thread your needle with two colors, or try a double needle. But remember to check that your double needle will fall inside the hole of the plate when setting it on zigzag.

Project
Buttons and Pendants

The following one-of-a-kind projects include free machining and stitching with feed dogs up. Get to know your sewing machine by stitching up these small embroideries.

You have a choice of stitches on the designs and they can be finished as large buttons (Figs. 2.6 and 2.7). Buy button forms at fabric or needlecraft shops. I used a size 75, which is about 2″ (5.1cm) in diameter. And I was inspired by Mary Ann Spawn of Tacoma, Washington, to finish some of

Stitch width: 0–2
Stitch length: 0–1/2
Needle position: center
Needle: #90/14 sharp
Feed dogs: up, lowered or covered
Presser foot: open embroidery and darning foot
Tension: *top*, loosened; *bobbin*, normal
Fabric suggestion: medium-weight, tightly woven linen
Thread: rayon embroidery in many colors
Accessories: wood or spring hoop, button forms or cardboard, batting, craft glue, cord, water-erasable pen, small beads (optional), colored markers, tracing paper, dressmaker's carbon, empty ballpoint pen
Stabilizer: tear-away or iron-on freezer paper

Fig. 2.6 Use button forms or cut shapes from heavy cardboard to make machine-embroidered pendants or buttons.

them by attaching cords and tassels to make pendants (Figs. 2.8 and 2.9).

If you use the round design, draw two circles with the same center point on your fabric. One is the area to be embroidered; the other circle, ½" (12.7mm) outside the first, is the cutting line. It's important to keep the area between the lines free from stitching. Use a piece of fabric large enough to go into a spring hoop and place a piece of tear-away stabilizer underneath.

Embroider, using free machining such as whipping and darning, as well as satin stitches. Leave a ½" (12.7mm) margin on the other designs as well. For each, trace the designs on linen fabric. The threads are rayon because I liked the contrast between the linen and the shiny threads.

On small embroidered pendants, I find it much easier to imitate the decorative built-in stitches than to actually use them. This way I can fudge a little on the designs, either shortening or elongating them, or making them wider or narrower to fit the space. Of course you can use built-in decorative stitches if you prefer.

Before I begin any pendant, I plan my colors by drawing the design on a piece of paper and coloring it. Once I begin stitching, not only do I sometimes change my mind about the placement of some colors, but I may add others and combine some by sewing next to or on top of the first threads I've used.

First, find the colored threads you'll need and then wind bobbins for all the

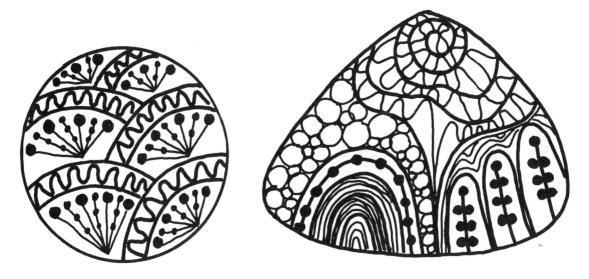

Fig. 2.7 Patterns for embroidered buttons or pendants, shown in Fig. 2.6.

Fig. 2.8 Use whip stitches to make a pendant using this pattern.

Fig. 2.9 Pattern for a rectangular machine-embroidered pendant.

spools of colors you'll use. If you want to add small beads to any of the pendants, keep them well within the outline.

General directions for making the three pendants follow: For the round, tasseled pendant, stretch your fabric (I used a natural linen) in a hoop and, using a water-erasable marker, draw in your design. Of course you can trace it from the book, but it is quite easily done free-hand—as are the others. Then place the hoop under the needle and slip stabilizer under the hoop. Begin stitching by freely "drawing" in the little flowers. (I used greens for the leaf and stem parts, oranges and yellows for the flowers.) When completed, change your machine to feed dogs up, embroidery foot on, satin stitch at 2 width. With a thread slightly darker than the linen, start at the top of the design and stitch in all the curved lines. The undulating lines between are whip stitches—the bobbin thread is brought to the top and covers the spool thread in the nubby texture I prefer to flat stitches. I also made sure I didn't cover the entire surface with stitches. Why cover a beautiful fabric completely? And also, I think that when fabric is completely hidden by machine embroidery, it looks too much like the appliqués you can pick up at the dime store.

All of the stitches on the triangular pendant are freely done whip-stitches.

I've included one other small rectangular pendant, combining piecing (the dark bottom area on the rectangle) with satin stitches and an area of free stitching. The circle is done freely, starting at the outside edge and working to the inside.

Pendants and buttons are small enough to do quickly and, if you make a mistake, they're easily disposable. There are no two alike. What a delightful way to spend an afternoon—stitching and getting to know your sewing machine.

When you've finished embroidering, cut out the shapes. Use large button forms for the round ones, or cut cardboard shapes to fit your embroidery. Place a piece of batting between your embroidery and the cardboard. Then make an identical circle, triangle or rectangle of plain fabric, batting and cardboard the same way. Use a thick craft glue to glue the fabric edges over the cardboard pieces. Then join back-to-back by dabbing glue between and whipping around the edge by hand. Add tassels if you wish.

By hand, stitch monk's cord around the join of the pendant for a beautiful finish. That same cord can be extended to tie around your neck. Or measure a length of monk's cord (see Chapter 10), and tie an overhand knot at each end. Stitch the knots to the top or sides of the pendants by hand.

CHAPTER 3

Adding Texture to Your Fabric

- **Lesson 3. Building up sewing stitches**
- **Lesson 4. Applying thick threads from top and bobbin**
- **Lesson 5. Fringing yarn and fabric**
- **Lesson 6. Adding buttons, beads, shisha**
- **Lesson 7. Smocking and gathering**
- **Lesson 8. Pulling threads together**

Add to or create texture on fabrics by building up sewing stitches, using thick threads, attaching fringe or objects like buttons and beads, gathering fabric for smocking or for utilitarian purposes—to stitch elastic on sleeves or bodices, or to make ruffles for curtains.

You'll make samples for your notebook; stitch up a fabric greeting card; cable stitch a tote bag square; make fabric fringe for rugs and doll hair; and make a framed picture. Both projects and samples will suggest numerous other ways to use these stitches.

Lesson 3. Building up sewing stitches

One of the simplest ways to build up texture is to sew in one place many times. Sounds simple and it is. But you can do this in so many ways that even though it is simple, the results aren't. Texture can look studied and exact or free and wild.

I use the following techniques for landscapes, monograms, and flowers. Practice each one for your notebook, recording your machine settings and any notes on how you might use the stitches later.

Begin with my suggested settings, but change them if they are not correct for your machine or not to your liking.

With the feed dogs up, and embroidery foot on, anchor the threads first; then use the widest satin stitch. Sew a block of 6 or 8 satin stitches. Anchor them by using 0 width again and stitch in place. Move the

> Stitch width: widest
> Stitch length: 0–1/2
> Needle position: left
> Needle: #90
> Feed dogs: up, lowered or covered
> Presser foot: darning or embroidery foot
> Tension: *top,* loosened; *bottom,* normal
> Fabric suggestion: experiment with varied weights, types, and colors
> Thread: practice with any type, but use machine embroidery thread for good; include several sizes of pearl cotton, cordonnet, yarns and ⅛" (3.2mm) ribbon
> Accessories: 7" (17.8cm) spring hoop
> Stabilizer: tear-away type

hoop and do another block of satin stitches. Keep them quite close together, but all at different angles (Fig. 3.1). Use these to fill in areas in designs (see Figs. 2.8 and 3.29).

Fig. 3.1 Use satin stitches for flower centers or fill-in background stitches.

For the next sample, lower or cover the feed dogs and use the darning foot. Anchor the threads by stitching in one place. Use the same wide zigzag, but sew in one place to build up 10 or 12 stitches. Move to another spot close to the first blob of stitches and stitch again. If you wish to achieve the effect in Fig. 3.2, pull the threads into

Fig. 3.2 Blobs and loops.

loops as you move from place to place and don't cut them off. You can make flower centers this way. Or finish by clipping between the satin stitches and then, using a different color on top, outlining with straight stitches (Fig. 3.3). Using variegated thread is especially effective.

Fig. 3.3 Straight-stitching around blobs.

In the next experiment, with feed dogs up, place the embroidery foot on, and set your machine on the widest satin stitch. Anchor the threads and sew a block of satin stitches at the left of the practice fabric. Pull the fabric down about three inches and over to the right slightly. Stitch another block of satin stitches. Pull up and over a bit to the right to stitch another block of satin stitches. Pull down and over for the third block. Continue across the fabric. Change threads and come back with another color. Cross the threads from the first pass as you do (Fig. 3.4). This is a good

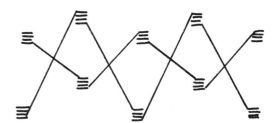

Fig. 3.4 Crossed threads and satin stitches.

filler for garden pictures—the stitches become hedges of flowers—or use layers of these to crown trees (Fig. 3.5).

Speaking of flowers, try the ones in Fig. 3.6, with feed dogs lowered or covered, using the same machine settings. Anchor the threads. Stitch one blob of about 10 or 12

22

glass with a water-erasable marker. With feed dogs lowered, anchor the thread and make a satin stitch blob perpendicular to the edge of the circle. Pull the thread across to the other side of the circle and make another blob. Anchor it. Cut off the thread. Go to another place on, just within, or just without the circle and stitch another blob. Pull the thread over to the other side, make another satin stitch blob, anchor it, and cut off the thread. Begin again and continue until you have made a flower head.

Now you'll practice filling in shapes, another way to bring texture to your base fabric. Zigzagging is probably the most widely used method to fill in designs. You can use any stitch width, but the wider the setting, the looser the look. I feel I have more control if I use a 2 width—or better yet, I sew with straight stitches to fill in

satin stitches in one place and, ending on the left side, the needle still in the fabric, turn the hoop. Do another blob and end on the left side. Turn the hoop and do another and another. Lay in about five or six of these to create a satin-stitch flower. The satin stitches will all have that common center—at needle left.

Make the next satin stitch flower (Fig. 3.7) by first tracing around a drinking

Fig. 3.6 Zigzag star flowers.

Fig. 3.7 Create flowers using zigzag stitches and crossed threads.

backgrounds. It is more like drawing with a pencil.

The drawback to straight-stitch filling is that the stitches are very tight to the fabric. Sometimes I want a lighter, loopier look, so I may start with zigzagging to fill in a design and then draw on top of that with straight stitches to emphasize a color, to outline, or to add shading to my embroidery. So I've included three ways to add texture to fabric by filling in designs with zigzag stitches.

Method A

In this method you will follow the contour of your design with zigzag stitches, changing a flat circle into a ball shape.

Stitch width: widest
Stitch length: 0
Needle position: center
Needle: #90
Feed dogs: lowered or covered
Presser foot: darning foot or use a wooden hoop with no foot
Tension: *top,* slightly loosened; *bobbin,* normal
Fabric suggestion: medium-weight cotton
Thread: sewing thread for practice
Accessories: large hoop at least 7" (17.8cm); water-erasable marker

Using the marker, draw several circles on the fabric in the hoop (I drew around the base of a large spool of thread). Place stabilizer under the hoop. Zigzag the first circle into a ball shape by stitching in curved lines. To make it easier, first draw stitching guidelines inside the circle (Fig. 3.8, method A, *left*).

Start at the top of the circle, stitching and moving your hoop sideways and back while following the curves you've drawn (Fig. 3.8, method A, *right*). Move from top to bottom, creating the ball shape as you stitch. Don't build up stitches too fast in one place. Move the hoop evenly, slowly, and practice coordination.

Try other stitch widths on the other circles you've drawn. Put the samples in your notebook.

Method B

This has been described as the stair-step method. Designs can be filled in by zigzag stitching from lower-left corner to upper-right corner and back again (Fig. 3.8, method B). To practice this, set up your machine as you did in method A. Draw sev-

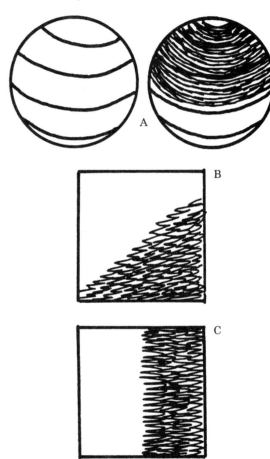

Fig. 3.8 Filling in designs with zigzag stitches. A. Draw guidelines in the circles, then move sideways and back, following the guidelines. B. Stair-step method. C. Encroaching zigzag.

eral 1½" (3.8cm) squares on your fabric. Although you will start with the widest stitch, experiment with other widths as you did before. Each line of zigzags blends into the one before it. Add your experiments to your notebook.

Method C

Encroaching zigzag is another way to fill in a design (Fig. 3.8, method C). Set up your machine as follows:

Stitch width: widest
Stitch length: 0
Needle position: center
Needle: #90
Feed dogs: lowered or covered
Presser foot: darning foot or no foot
Tension: *top,* slightly loosened; *bobbin,* normal

Fabric: medium-weight cotton
Thread: sewing thread for practice
Accessories: 7" (17.8cm) hoop, tear-away stabilizer, water-erasable marker

This time, draw only one 2" (5.1cm) square on the fabric in the hoop, and place stabilizer under it. Keep the hoop in the same position in front of you; don't rotate it. Instead, move it backward and forward as you stitch. Start at the top of the right side of the square you've drawn and stitch down to the bottom, moving the hoop slowly to keep the stitches close together. Move the hoop to the left a bit and stitch back up to the top, overlapping the first stitching slightly. Continue until you have covered the square. Go back and stitch on top of stitches for more texture. Do a sample for your notebook.

Lesson 4. Applying thick threads from the top and bobbin

We created texture with regular sewing threads in Lesson 3, but in this lesson we'll change sewing and machine-embroidery threads for thicker threads, such as pearl cotton, cordonnet, and crocheted cotton. We'll explore four different ways to create texture by attaching these thick threads to fabric, including using them on the top spool, couched down on top of fabric, threaded up through the hole in the throat plate of the machine, and wound on the bobbin.

Adding texture adds interest to sewing and embroidery. Perhaps it's not essential—a dress is still a dress without textured decoration—but it is a long-cut, that something extra that takes your dress from ordinary to special. Adding cords, fringe, objects, and gathers to the background fabric are all easy techniques once you know your machine.

Applying thick thread through the needle

Thread as large as cordonnet can be sewn with a #110 needle. Topstitching needles also have eyes to accommodate double threads or thick threads like buttonhole twist, and are available in #80–#110 needles.

Whatever you use, the thread must slip through the needle easily and the needle must make a hole in the fabric large enough to keep the thread from fraying.

Couching thread down on top of fabric

If thread is too thick for the needle, try couching it down on top of the fabric using a cording foot. Pull cord through the hole, front to back, and tie a knot at the back of your cord to keep from losing it before you begin. If you use a cording foot, as soon as you start stitching the thread will be fed through this hole with no help needed. It will stay exactly in place as you satin stitch over it with a zigzag or other decorative stitch. Cover the cord as closely or sparsely as you wish, using different stitch lengths.

You can substitute other feet—pintuck, hemmer (zigzag), appliqué, invisible zipper foot or braiding foot. You may need to change needle position, depending upon which foot you use. Unlike the cording foot which feeds the thread automatically, you may have to guide the cord if you use one of the other feet mentioned.

Because of this, I feel that owning a cording foot is mandatory. I couldn't sew without it. Covering cord is just one use. I also use it without cord when I want to sew a perfectly straight line of stitches. The center hole is a perfect guide when I line it up with the stitching line on my fabric. If a cording foot isn't available for your machine, check the Sources of Supply list and order a generic one.

Try multiple cords as well. There is a special foot available with holes for the cords, or use a foot with a wide groove underneath like an embroidery foot. Also, try the braiding foot or a pintuck foot for this purpose.

Project
Greeting Card

Practice applying thick threads on top of the fabric by making the greeting card shown in Fig. 3.9.

Use the pattern in Fig. 3.10 as a guide, changing measurements to fit the card folder or frame. Trace the pattern from the book, then place the drawing on top of the white background fabric, with dressmaker's carbon between. Transfer it, using the empty ballpoint pen.

Stitch width: 0–4
Stitch length: 1/2–2
Needle position: center
Needle: #90
Feed dogs: up, down or covered
Presser foot: appliqué or embroidery foot, bulky overlock, edging foot, darning foot
Tension: *top*, loosened; *bobbin*, normal
Fabric suggestions: 12″ (30.5cm) square of white polished cotton, 6″ (15.2cm) square of green polished cotton, 12″ (30.5cm) square of yellow organdy
Thread: rayon in rainbow colors—yellow, red, green, purple, blue; #3 pearl cotton in the same colors; monofilament
Accessories: 7″ (17.8cm) spring hoop; circle maker or thumb tack, transparent tape, cork or eraser; water-erasable pen; greeting card folder (available at craft, art, and needlework shops) or picture frame; dressmaker's carbon; empty ballpoint pen
Stabilizer: tear-away

Cut a piece from the green fabric large enough for the area at the bottom of the design, plus 1″ (2.5cm). Fold under the top edge of the green about ½″ (12.7mm) and press it. Hold it in place with pins and apply it using the edging foot, with monofilament thread on the top and bobbin, and the machine set on a blind hem stitch—stitch width 1, stitch length 2.

Next, stretch three layers of yellow organdy over the white and green fabric and put them all in a spring hoop. Back this with tear-away. Set up the circle maker on your machine. (If you don't have a circle maker, use the thumb tack method in Fig. 1.2.) Poke the tack through at the center of the three layers of organdy. Place the appliqué presser foot on the line of the inner circle. Stitch on that line around the circle

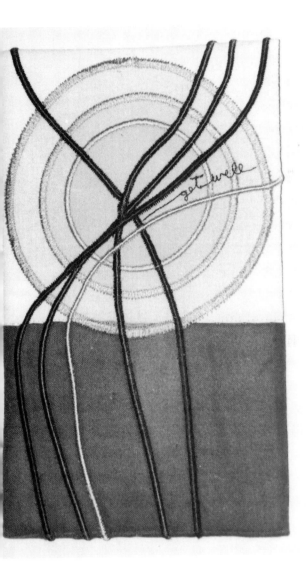

Fig. 3.9 "Even the Rainbow is Upset" greeting card.

2, length 1/2, or the setting on your machine for smooth, close satin stitches.

Then move the tack so the line of the next circle will be centered under your presser foot. Straight stitch around the circle, cut back and satin stitch again as you did with the first. Do the same for the last layer of organdy.

Take the fabric out of the hoop while you stitch over the cords, but place tear-away stabilizer underneath. Each cord is a different color; use a presser foot like Bernina's bulky overlock to guide the pearl cotton. If you don't have one, then use an embroidery foot, zigzag hemmer, or appliqué foot. After fitting the pearl cotton into the grooves, you will guide it as you stitch. You may have to change needle positions to cover the cord perfectly. Stitch over the cords, using close satin stitches. I prefer to stitch in two passes, attaching the cord first, then stitching in close satin stitches to cover it evenly and smoothly on the second pass.

When the last cord has been covered, change to the darning foot, feed dogs down or covered, straight stitch. Use the color you have on your machine — unless it's yellow — to write a message along the top of one of the cords. I wrote "get well," and on the inside I'll write the message: "Even the rainbow is upset."

Finish the edge with a straight stitch. Trim close to stitches and slip into the card folder or finish it for a framed picture.

Also try the bulky overlock foot for sewing down bulky yarn or cords invisibly. Choose either the overlock stitch or the blind hemming stitch (Fig. 3.11). Set up your machine as follows:

Stitch width: 1 1/2
Stitch length: 1 1/2
Needle position: half right (blind hem
    stitch); half left (overlock stitch)
Needle: varies
Feed dogs: up
Presser foot: bulky overlock, open embroidery foot, or zigzag hemmer

with a straight stitch. Take the fabric out of the hoop and cut back only the top layer of organdy to the stitching.

Place the greeting card back in the hoop, with the tack back in its original hole. Satin stitch with the machine set on a width of

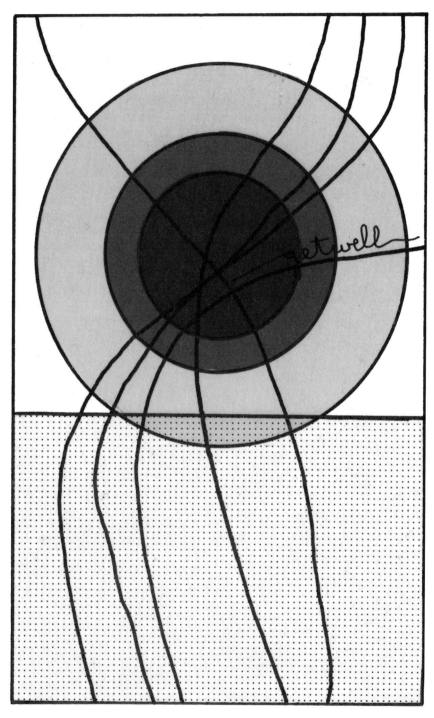

Fig. 3.10 Greeting card pattern. Enlarge or reduce to fit your card folder.

Tension: *top,* normal; *bobbin,* normal
Thread: monofilament on top, polyester
    on bobbin
Stabilizer: tear-away

Stitch alongside the cord. At the wide bite of the needle, the cord is sewn down with a tiny, almost unnoticeable stitch. When the line of stitching is completed, go back and gently nudge the cord over toward the stitching line. Now your monofilament will be completely hidden.

Or, using a bulky overlock, open embroidery, or multi-cord foot, line up several threads of pearl cotton next to each other. Use a zigzag or built-in stitch to attach them with monofilament or with a colored thread. Make colorful shoelaces this way.

Soutache is like a thick cord, and can be attached perfectly using a braiding foot. It is not easily done without this special foot, as there is no way to hold the braid in place so the needle will enter exactly in the center each time. It's sometimes possible to feed other cords, narrow braids or rickrack through the hole in this foot. To attach soutache, trace the design on the topside of your fabric, using a water-erasable pen. Place stabilizer under the fabric.

Corners are not impossible if you walk the machine around them. Stop at the corner, needle down, presser foot raised. Turn the fabric 45 degrees, lower the foot, take one stitch; then, needle down again, raise the presser foot, turn the fabric to complete the corner. You'll get a good angle. If you can, though, choose a design with undulating curves, which are easier to accomplish.

Use soutache and other braids down jacket and vest fronts, around sleeves, to decorate belts and handbags.

If the braid crosses and recrosses itself, threading in and out like a Celtic interlacing cord, it is still possible to use the braiding foot. The braid will not be threaded through the foot, but will be hand basted in place on the fabric, then fit within the groove as you carefully ride over it and stitch it down.

For your next sample, use a darning foot for wool when freely couching down yarn. This darning foot may have a guide in the front to hold the yarn as you freely attach it. To get the feel of the foot, use straight lines or gentle curves on your first samples. Try a smooth, sport-weight yarn for your first experiment. Add the result to your growing notebook.

Here's another invisible way to attach thick, twisted cord or yarn to fabric (Fig. 3.12). Leave the machine set up for free machining, but remove the presser foot or use a darning foot. Use monofilament thread on top. Iron a piece of freezer paper onto the back of the fabric. Begin by drawing the bobbin thread to the top and anchoring the threads. Stitch the end of the cord down. Then move along one side of the cord with a straight stitch. When you reach a twist in the cord, follow it to the other side by stitching in the twist. Once

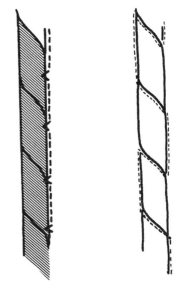

Fig. 3.11 Use the blind-hem stitch to attach cord invisibly.

Fig. 3.12 Stitch alongside, then across the twist, to attach cord.

on the other side, follow along that side for a few stitches until you reach the top of the next twist. Cross over again, following the twist. Continue in this manner until the cord is attached.

Attaching cord pulled through the needleplate

You can also attach thick cords to the surface of fabric by threading them through the hole in the needleplate on some machines, or through an attachment placed at the front of the needleplate on others. Purchase a needleplate (See Sources of Supply) if you don't have one. Sometimes holes can be drilled in the plate you have to accommodate cord and elastic. Of course, this method attaches the cord underneath the fabric so you must stitch with the top-side of the fabric against the needleplate.

Once you have the cord threaded through the hole, tie a knot at the end so it does not slip out again.

I've used this method of attaching cords through the needleplate for collages, when I want to add long lines of thick cords easily and fast. I draw on the stabilizer, which is on top of the wrong side of the fabric, to indicate where I should stitch. The cord is fed evenly through the plate and attached to the fabric with straight or zigzag stitches.

Stitch a record of your experiments with straight stitch and zigzag. Also try cord through the needleplate with some of the built-in stitches intended for decorative edgings, like the scallop stitch.

You can also apply round elastic with this method.

Use pearl cotton through the needleplate for pintucking with double needles (see Chapter 5). Make samples using each pintuck foot you own. Stitch many rows, spacing them according to the spacing on the pintuck feet. Mark them for your notebook.

Using thick thread from the bobbin

Cable stitching is an embroidery technique using thick thread on the bobbin. The topside of the fabric will be against the bed of the machine. It can be done with feed dogs up, using an embroidery foot for straight or built-in stitches, or it can be done freely with feed dogs down or covered, using a darning foot or using no presser foot at all.

Cabling can look like a tightly couched thread or like fluffy fur, depending on the thread you choose. A hard twist thread like crochet cotton will lay flatter, with less beading or looping than a soft, loosely twisted yarn like mohair. The effects you get will depend not only on top and bobbin tension, but on stitch width, stitch length, color and size of cord, color of top thread, feed dogs up or down, color, weight, and type of fabric, how fast you stitch and how fast you move the hoop.

When I say you can use thick threads, I'm not kidding. Did you know that you can use up to a four-ply yarn in the bobbin? Of course, the thicker the yarn, the less you can wind on the bobbin. Usually the bobbin can be put on the machine and wound slowly while you hold the yarn or cord to control it. If you find the yarn must be wound by hand, do so evenly without stretching it.

To use the thicker threads this embroidery requires, you must override that panicky feeling that accompanies loosening and tightening the tension on the bobbin. Perhaps you've already discovered, as you've changed bobbins, that you can recognize the feel of normal tension. If not (and if you have a removable bobbin case), put a bobbin full of sewing thread into the bobbin case and click the thread into the spring. Hold on to the end of the thread and let the bobbin case hang from it like a yoyo. It should drop slowly when jerked.

Memorize how this feels with normal tension before you begin to loosen the bobbin spring for cabling. Loosen the spring over an empty box, as the screw has a tendency to pop out and disappear forever. I've purchased several extra screws just in case.

On built-in bobbin cases you will either dial down to a lower number (it is easy then to return to normal tension by returning to the original number) or by turning a screw in the machine. Mark the location of the slot on the screw to return it to normal tension.

When adjusting tension for heavy threads, remember that the cord must feed through the bobbin case smoothly. Loosen the bobbin tension by turning the screw counter-clockwise until the tension feels normal to you.

If you have a built-in bobbin case, turn the dial counter-clockwise to loosen it. Refer to your manual and experiment with the setting.

For both built-in and removable bobbins, you may have to bypass the tension spring altogether if the cord or yarn is too thick.

Practice cabling on a piece of scrap fabric. Set up your machine with feed dogs up, using an embroidery thread on top or regular sewing thread. Place your fabric in a hoop and use an open embroidery foot. Stitch and then look under the fabric to be sure the tension is set correctly—do you want tight, stiff stitches or loosely looping ones? Manipulate the bobbin tension for different effects.

Don't forget the top tension. It must be loose enough so the bobbin thread stays underneath the fabric; but if it is too loose, it may keep the stitches from staying neatly in place.

Write on your sample fabric which is the topside, which the back. Also record bobbin and top spool tensions by using + and − signs.

Most embroiderers I know, if they own machines with removable bobbin cases, buy extra bobbin cases to use for embroidery only. Buying an extra case is a good idea. It's possible to tighten and loosen the spring screw—or even remove the spring altogether—without the time-consuming adjustments needed to return to normal sewing tension.

Whatever you choose to do, don't be afraid of your sewing machine. Change tensions, lengths, speeds, and use it to its full potential. Get to know your machine.

Now prepare a cabling sample for your notebook. Choose a medium-weight cotton or blend. Use all the built-in stitches with #3, #5, and then #8 pearl cotton. Try ribbon and yarn as well. Keep the stitch long enough to prevent the cord from bunching up under the fabric. Open built-in stitches work best and simple zigzag is most effective. I like the zigzag opened up to a 2 or 3 length and a 4 stitch width. It gives a rick-rack effect.

Stretch a piece of fabric in a hoop, but don't use a stabilizer underneath. Instead, use a stabilizer on top to keep your stitches from pulling. Draw lines or designs on the stabilizer. This is actually the back of your work.

Dip the needle into the fabric, drawing the bobbin thread or cord to the top. Hold the threads to the side as you begin. If you can't bring the cord up through the fabric, then pierce the cloth with an awl or large needle and bring it up. Don't anchor the threads with a lockstitch at the beginning or end. Instead, pull the threads to the back each time you start; when you stop, leave a long enough tail to be able to thread it up in a hand-sewing needle and poke it through to the back. Later you can work these threads into the stitching by hand.

It is also possible to quilt with this technique. Using a white pearl cotton in the bobbin and a top thread to match the fabric, you can get an effect which looks much like Japanese Sashiko (Fig. 3.13).

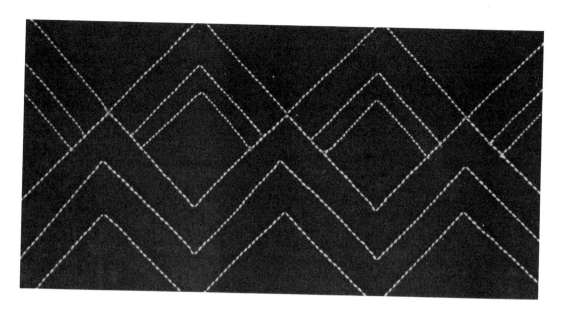

Fig. 3.13 Stitching in the style of Japanese Sashiko.

Apply ⅛″ (3.2mm) double-faced satin ribbon as shown in Fig. 3.14. Wind the ribbon onto the bobbin. Only machines that require winding bobbins inside the machine cannot sew on ribbon using this method. The end of the ribbon will bypass the tension spring. Then place the bobbin in the case. Use the regular presser foot, needle right, stitch length about 4 or use a topstitch setting.

When you start and stop in this type of couching, the ribbon is brought to the underside and finished off by hand. This technique is used on the infant's bonnet in Chapter 5.

Next try cabling with free embroidery. Place a medium-weight fabric in a hoop with a stabilizer on top. Lower or cover the feed dogs and, using a darning foot or bare needle, freely straight stitch, then zigzag.

Plan the lines of stitching before you begin. As you work, sew and peek under your hoop so you can regulate the bobbin and top tensions to your liking. Practice turn-

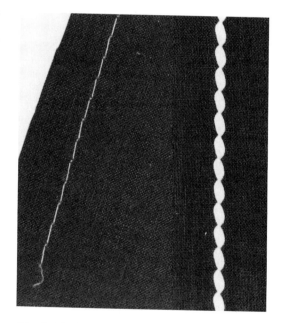

Fig. 3.14 The top and underneath of a ribbon attached by machine stitching.

ing, pushing and pulling the hoop, sewing circles and straight lines. When your stitching changes direction, the tension is also changed, so practice how fast you should move your hoop for the effects you want. Often a design can be seen from the back of printed fabric. Take advantage of that to stitch a sample piece for your notebook. Stretch the fabric in a hoop. Water-soluble stabilizer can be used underneath if the fabric is washable. Otherwise, don't use a stabilizer. Instead, be sure your fabric is very taut, and use the darning foot. Embellish these prints by outlining the designs with pearl cotton or thick rayon thread on the bobbin.

Use bridal veiling as your fabric and create original lace. Or, decorate velveteen using velour yarn on the bobbin and monofilament thread on the top.

Project
Tote Bag
Square (Cabling)

Think "spring" with a tote bag square; the pattern is provided in Fig. 3.15. Remember that directions for making the tote and finishing the squares are in Chapter 12.

Transfer the design in Fig. 3.15 to tracing paper and then, using dressmaker's carbon and the ballpoint pen, transfer the design to freezer paper. Color in or mark each flower to indicate color. Press this to the underside of your fabric. Always do a sample first, using the same fabric, stabilizer and threads as you will be using on your finished copy. Peek under the sample and adjust the tensions as needed. When cabling, you always work with underside up.

Use green machine embroidery thread on the spool and bobbin. With feed dogs up, zigzag foot on, tensions normal, straight stitch the "stem" lines in first, stitch length 2. When you come to a flower, raise the presser foot and pull across to the other side. Continue stitching.

Change to feed dogs lowered or covered, darning foot on, bobbin tension loosened (until normal for #5 pearl cotton). Use a green pearl cotton bobbin with green on the spool. Pull the thick pearl to the top, but don't anchor it at the beginning or at the end. Stitch across the square, following the thick green lines. Pull across the flowers as you did with the green thread. When finished, turn over and clip out the cords and threads that stretch across the flowers.

Stitch the flower centers with the green pearl bobbin and green machine-embroidery spool. Don't anchor the threads at the beginning or the end. Leave ends long enough to poke the thick thread to the back and work into the stitches there later.

To stitch circles, always start at the outer edge and work toward the middle. Stitch

Stitch width: 0 to wide satin stitch
Stitch length: 0–2
Needle position: center
Needle: #80
Feed dogs: up, lowered or covered
Presser foot: darning, zigzag
Tension: *top,* normal; *bobbin,* normal, then loosened for #5 pearl cotton
Fabric suggestions: 9″-square medium-weight white fabric
Thread: green, peach, orange and yellow machine embroidery thread (or try variegated threads in these colors); three bobbins wound with #5 pearl cotton (peach, yellow, orange), two bobbins wound with green #5 pearl cotton
Accessories: tracing paper, dressmaker's carbon, empty ballpoint pen, water-erasable pen
Stabilizer: freezer paper

Fig. 3.15 Pattern for tote bag square.

as closely as you can to the stitching you have just put in until you have reached the center.

Then, using peach, yellow and orange pearl cotton, stitch in the flowers as you did the green centers. Begin each of the flowers by stitching on top of the cut ends of the green pearl cotton at each side to hide and anchor the green cords.

When you've finished, pull off the freezer paper and work in the pearl cotton beginnings and ends by hiding them in the stitches on the underside. Finish as explained in Chapter 12.

Lesson 5. Fringing yarn and fabric

In this lesson you will learn to make fringe with a fringing fork, as well as with strips of fabric sewn together and clipped into fringe. Start by using a fringing fork to make yarn fringe. It can be used for wigs, costumes, rugs, and decorating edges of garments. Fringing forks are available in many different sizes. Or, you can make

```
Stitch width: 4
Stitch length: 1
Needle position: center
Feed dogs: up
Presser foot: open embroidery foot
Tension: top, normal; bobbin, normal
Fabric suggestion: 1"-wide (2.5cm-
     wide) bias strips, several yards
Thread: polyester to match bias
Accessories: large fringe fork
Stabilizer: adding machine tape
```

yarn feeds off

start wrapping

A

B   C

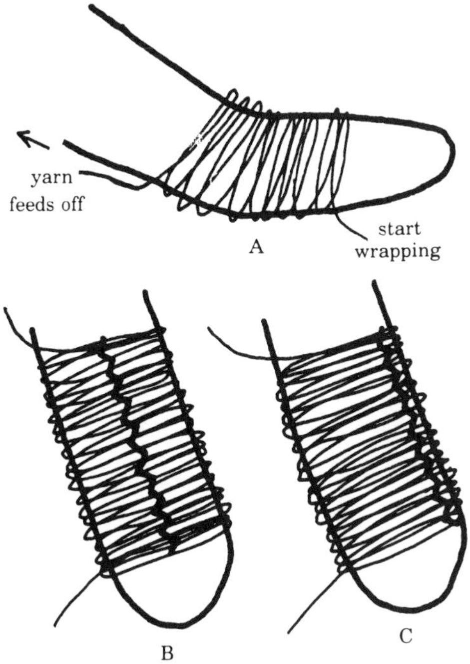

Fig. 3.16 The fringe fork. A. Wrap with yarn or fabric strips. B. Sew down in the middle. C. Or sew at the side of the fork for wider fringe.

your own using wire, ranging from the thickness of a coat hanger to fine as a hairpin.

Wrap the fork as shown in Fig. 3.16, sew down the center, pull the loops toward you, and wrap some more. If making yards and yards of fringe, use Robbie Fanning's method of measuring. Robbie measures the length she wants from a roll of adding-machine tape and stitches her fringe right to the tape. This also keeps the fringe from twisting. When you're finished, tear off the paper and apply the fringe.

Sometimes you may not want the fringe sewn in the middle (Fig. 3.16A). Stitch it at the edge of the fork to make fringe twice as wide as that made by sewing down the center (Fig. 3.16B). As you work with the fork, you will understand when to use each method. And don't limit yourself to yarn or string alone. Try fabric. I used it for doll hair for my denim doll.

I wrapped the fork with red denim and

Fig. 3.17 The doll's hair is fabric fringe, her eyelashes are thread fringe done with the tailor-tacking foot.

sewed down the center over adding-machine tape. When I had enough for hair, I tore the paper off the fringe and pinned the hair to her head in various ways to decide what hairdo I liked best. I sewed it on by hand; I could have left it as it was, but I decided to clip the loops (Fig. 3.17).

But you can achieve almost the same effect with fabric without using the fringing fork. Work with strips of fabrics, but don't clip them into fringe until after they are sewn to the item you are making.

Project
Fringed Denim Rug

This fabric-fringe project, a little rug, ate up yards of old jeans and denim remnants I picked up at sales; I kept cutting 2½″ (6.4cm) strips on the bias until I had finished the rug.

You'll need a piece of heavy fabric the size of the finished rug, plus an inch all around. Measure the perimeter and cut a piece of 1″-wide (2.5cm-wide) fusible webbing. Using a Teflon pressing sheet, press the fusible webbing to the topside of all the

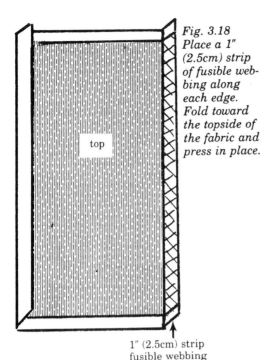

Fig. 3.18 Place a 1" (2.5cm) strip of fusible webbing along each edge. Fold toward the topside of the fabric and press in place.

top

1" (2.5cm) strip
fusible webbing

Stitch width: 0
Stitch length: 2
Needle position: right
Needle: jeans needle
Presser foot: zipper
Tension: *top,* normal; *bobbin,* normal
Fabric suggestion: denim, cut into 2½" (6.4cm) bias strips of blues and red; use remnants and old jeans to cut quantity needed for rug size you want; heavy upholstery fabric for rug backing
Thread: matching polyester thread
Stabilizer: 1"-wide (2.5cm-wide) fusible webbing (measure circumference of rug)

Fig. 3.20 The bias strips are clipped into fringe.

Fig. 3.19 Stitching bias strips onto the rug.

edges and fold them back on the topside of the fabric, pressing again (Fig. 3.18). This is the top of the rug, so the edges will be finished when the last strip is stitched down.

Fold the first bias strip lengthwise to find the center, but open it again and place

it ⅛" (3.5mm) from the edge of the upholstery fabric. Stitch down the center crease of each strip from top to bottom (Fig. 3.19). Fold the left side of the strip to the right. Push the next strip as close as you can get it to the first. Sew down the center again; Fig. 3.19 shows the first three fabric strips stitched down. If you run out of fabric for a strip, add another by overlapping the last strip at least 1" (2.5cm).

When you're all done stitching, clip each strip every ½" (12.7mm), staggering the clips for each row. My rug (Fig. 3.20) went into the washer and dryer to soften.

Lesson 6. Adding buttons, beads, shisha

Attaching buttons

Once you've attached a button by machine, you won't want to do it any other way, it is so speedy. If you are applying buttons to a garment you've made, be sure the button area is interfaced. Dab glue stick on the underside of the button and position it.

Place the button foot on top of the button and stitch in the hole to the left 3 or 4 times to anchor the threads (stitch width 0). Raise the needle and move the stitch width so the needle clears the button and falls into the hole at the right. On that setting, stitch back and forth several times. When you have finished, move the stitch width to 0 and anchor again. That's all there is to it. (Some machines do not have a button foot. Rather, they use the presser foot shank to hold the buttons in place. Check your manual).

Stitch width: space between holes in the button
Stitch length: 0
Needle position: far left
Needle: #80
Feed dogs: lowered
Presser foot: button, tailor tack, or overlock foot
Tension: *top,* normal; *bobbin,* normal
Thread: polyester
Accessories: Viking button reed, button elevator, or toothpick are optional, transparent tape, glue stick, scrap fabrics, buttons, beads and shisha mirrors (see Sources of Supply)

If the garment fabric is thick, such as coating, you will need to make a button shank; otherwise, the buttonhole will pucker whenever the coat is buttoned. Raise the stitches to create a shank by taping a darning needle or round toothpick between the holes on top of the button before you stitch (Fig. 3.21A). When finished, pull off the tape and remove the darning needle. Leave a long thread to wrap around the shank and anchor with a hand needle, strengthening the shank.

Or use the Viking button reed (Fig. 3.21B). It is a small gadget made to slip under the button to raise it off the fabric and create either of two shank heights. A button elevator, which accomplishes the same thing, is available at notion counters.

The tailor-tacking foot can also be used, but it will give you a very high shank, so experiment first.

Another foot to use for a higher shank is the overlock foot. Place the bar in the middle of the button, then adjust the needle position and stitch width as needed.

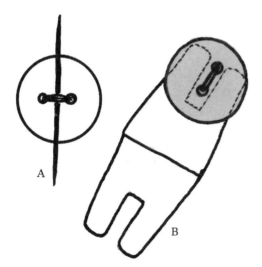

Fig. 3.21 Sew on a button with a shank.
A. Use a toothpick on top of the button.
B. Use the Viking button reed.

Attaching beads and baubles

Beads can be attached by machine if the hole in the bead is large enough and your needle fine enough. The thickness of the bead also matters if you zigzag it in place. Lower or cover the feed dogs, remove the presser foot, adjust the stitch width as di-

Fig. 3.22 If beads are stitched down on only one side, they can be nudged to stand up.

Fig. 3.23 Stitching down both sides to make beads lie flat.

rected. Hand-walk the machine first to see if the needle will clear the bead, and if the sizes of the bead and needle are compatible. If attaching the bead by hand-walking only, attach the rim of the bead to the fabric by first holding it in place with a dot of glue from a glue stick. Anchor the thread in the center of the bead by stitching in place three or four times. Raise the needle. Move the fabric over to anchor the thread on the side of the bead. Go back to the center and anchor again. Repeat until the bead is securely sewn in place and will stand up (Fig. 3.22). Nudge the bead to stand on its outside rim when you finish stitching. Wipe off the glue.

If you go back and stitch down the other side as well, your bead will lay flat, hole up (Fig. 3.23).

Attaching seed beads, or other fine or oddly shaped beads can be done in the following way. First string the beads onto a thread. Using monofilament, stitch one end of the beaded thread down on the fabric. Stitch along the thread the width of one bead. Push the first bead near that end and then stitch over the thread to keep the bead in place. Stitch again the distance of the next bead. Push the bead up to the first, stitch over the thread and repeat, as shown in Fig. 3.24.

Or sew beads down by stringing them singly on thick threads and stitching both ends of the threads down (Fig. 3.25).

You can attach beads invisibly, using monofilament thread to couch them down

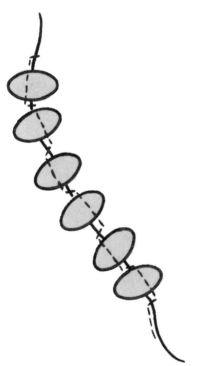

Fig. 3.24 A string of seed beads, attached by machine along dotted line (solid line is thread).

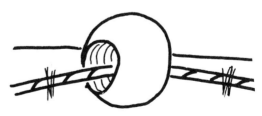

Fig. 3.25 Attach a large bead by threading a cord through it and stitching on either side of the cord.

Fig. 3.26 Using needlelace to attach beads.

or to string the beads on. Or choose your thread wisely and use the stitching as a part of the decoration.

Another way to hold down beads is to first stitch strips of needlelace on water-soluble stabilizer. When the lace has been stitched, merely pull off the excess stabilizer and hold your work under a faucet to wash out most of what remains, but leave a bit of the sticky residue. When it is almost dry, shape the needlelace strips and they will dry in that shape. Use two or

Fig. 3.27 "The Flop Box," made by Pat Pasquini, has a machine-embellished top by the author. It includes beads held down with needlelace, other beads strung with cord and porcupine quills and couched in place, textures created by stitching cords down, using a double needle to pintuck suede, and stitching blobs and satin stitches in the background. Photo by Robbie Fanning.

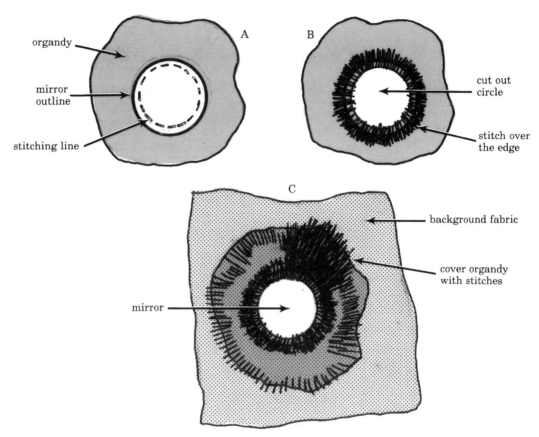

Labels on figure:

A:
organdy
mirror outline
stitching line

B:
cut out circle
stitch over the edge

C:
background fabric
cover organdy with stitches
mirror

Fig. 3.28 Glue the shisha to the background fabric. A. On organdy, stitch around a circle slightly smaller than the shisha. B. Cut out the center and embroider over the edge. C. Place the organdy over the shisha and stitch it in place on background fabric by straight stitching. Embroider the background to conceal the edge.

three of these strips to hold down beads or washers (Fig. 3.26). Thread a strip through the object and stitch down one end. Move the bauble down over your stitching. Arrange the strip, twisting it if you wish. Then stitch down the other end freely and invisibly. Use this method, as I have, on decorative box tops and collages (Fig. 3.27).

Another method of using stones and jewels for wall hangings or pictures is to cover them with net or transparent fabrics, and then stitch down the fabric. Then cut holes in the fabric large enough to let the objects show through and small enough so they don't fall out.

Or make needlelace in the center of wire bent into a circle, rectangle, or other shape. Stretch the lace over an object placed on a background fabric. Attach the lace to the fabric by stitching freely, close to the wire, around the inside of this frame, and cutting off the wire. Embroider the edges if you wish.

Attaching shisha mirrors

Shishas are small pieces of mirrored glass. They are about 1″ (2.5cm) in diameter, but are never exactly circular. It is possible to attach them to fabric if you follow the methods Caryl Rae Hancock of Indianapolis, and Gail Kibiger of Warsaw, Indiana, invented.

This is Caryl Rae Hancock's method, illustrated in Fig. 3.28. First, stretch organdy in a hoop. The shisha is placed on top of the organdy and its outline traced. The back of the shisha is dabbed with glue stick and placed on a background fabric, not the organdy.

Sew around—and about ⅛" (3.2mm) inside—the drawn circle. Stitch around two more times. Without taking the fabric out of the hoop, cut out the circle of fabric within the stitching. After anchoring threads, the machine should be set on a medium width zigzag and the circle stitched freely around the cut edge. Turn the hoop as you sew around it, letting the stitches radiate from the edge of the hole to about ½" (12.7mm) beyond. The organdy must be covered with stitches at this time. Anchor threads and take the organdy out of the hoop. Cut very closely around the outside stitching.

With the machine changed back to straight stitch, place the piece of embroidery over the shisha and background fabric and pin organdy in place. Stitch around outside edge of the shisha. Be careful: if you stitch into the glass, the needle and probably the shisha will break.

Leave the machine as set or change to zigzag again and stitch over those straight stitches, following the radiating direction of the original zigzagging. Blend the outside edge of the organdy with the background fabric by radiating stitches onto the background fabric.

Gail Kibiger has a slightly different method. She applies shisha by first placing the mirror on the background fabric, not on organdy, and tracing around it. Removing the shisha, she stitches ⅛" (3.2mm) within this circle three times and cuts out the circle. Gail embroiders on the back-

ground fabric as Caryl Rae did the organdy.

The shisha is then glued to a piece of organdy and placed under the finished hole. After pinning it in place, she straight stitches around the mirror to hold it in place.

One of Gail's variations is to work a spiderweb across the hole before the edges are zigzagged.

Silver bangles, the large sequins found in craft and knitting shops, are an excellent substitute for shisha. Not only are they exactly round, unlike the uneven shape of shishas, but they are durable. If you sew into them, your needle doesn't break. Make a record for your notebook of how you have applied buttons, beads and shishas.

Project Bird Collage

I work with transparent fabrics almost exclusively, so I collect them. Besides fabric stores, garage sales and thrift shops are wonderful sources. I check out the chiffon scarves, colored nylons, lingerie, curtains, as well as glitzy dresses—though it takes courage to buy some of these because of the double-takes at the checkout counter.

This is a beadwork project, which includes appliqué as well. Bird shapes are my favorites. I like them plump like baby chicks, sleek like soaring eagles, even whimsical like African Dahomey appliqués. I've used them on quilts, wall hangings, and in fabric collages.

In this small picture, shown in Fig. 3.29, I added small clay beads by machine to the appliquéd picture.

If this sounds overwhelming, you can substitute any colors you wish, and use only one, instead of a variety, of transparent fabrics. Although I used transparent thread for most of this collage, I added browns, greens and beiges in rayon stitches when my piece was almost complete.

Begin by pulling off a half-dozen threads from the square of background fabric. Cut these threads into small lengths of 1 and 2 inches (2.5–5.0cm) and add them to the other threads you've cut—you will need several dozen. Put them aside.

Iron freezer paper to the back of the linen fabric for stability, as you will not use a hoop for this project. Although not necessary, I always cut the background fabric at least 6″–8″ (15.2–20.3cm) bigger than the finished size so I can practice stitching or layering on the edges. Also, I plan my pieces so they look as if they go on beyond the frame. I don't want them to look as if they end inside it.

Fig. 3.30 shows the arrangement, and Fig. 3.31 is the pattern; cut out the fabric pieces as follows: Cut out the oval nest from the taupe fabric and place that slightly below the center on the background. When I cut fabric for collages, I use a cut/tear method. By pulling slightly on the fabric as I cut, I fray the material a bit to keep the edges soft. The bird should be cut from green suede or felt so it will not roll when you cut it out. Be sure to use fabric that has some body, so it will be easy to control. Place the bird on the nest (Fig. 3.30). Cut a gold wing from suede and posi-

Fig. 3.29 Bird collage.

Fig. 3.30 Follow this design for assembling the bird picture.

tion that on the bird. Cut out the transparent wings. Place one on top of the gold wing, but shift it a bit so it is not exactly in the same place as the first. Do the same with the other sheers. Your wings will cross, meet, blend, as if in a watercolor. Over the last wing you will use one cut from a yellow mesh grapefruit bag or a coarse yellow net. Rearrange until the wings look pleasing to you.

Cut the foot and top off a nude-colored nylon stocking and slit the stocking from top to bottom. Stretch it over the picture and pin it down just beyond the image area. As you stretch the stocking, it will lighten in color. It should be almost invisible, but not stretched so tightly it buckles the picture. This holds all the pieces in place, and softens, but does not change, the colors of your picture.

Lower or cover the feed dogs on your machine. Use a darning foot, as you will have many layers to stitch together. Begin by freely sewing around the bird with transparent thread. Stitch just off the edge of the body and wing pieces. It is not important to be completely accurate; it's fine if you stitch into the body or wings. You

44

Stitch width: 0–4
Stitch length: 0
Needle position: center
Needle: #90
Feed dogs: lowered
Presser foot: darning foot
Tension: *top,* slightly loosened; *bobbin,* normal
Fabric suggestions: green and gold suede or felt for bird's body and wings; transparent fabrics, such as organdy, chiffon, yellow mesh grapefruit bag, for the wings; moss green bridal veiling to cover the picture; 12″ (30.5cm) square of coarse beige upholstery linen for background; loosely woven taupe-colored fabric for the nest; gold lamé for the eggs; nude-colored nylon stocking; also needed are small clay beads
Thread: several strands of brown and beige coarse thread or string, cut into 1″ (2.5cm) pieces; brown, green and beige shiny rayon; monofilament
Stabilizer: freezer paper

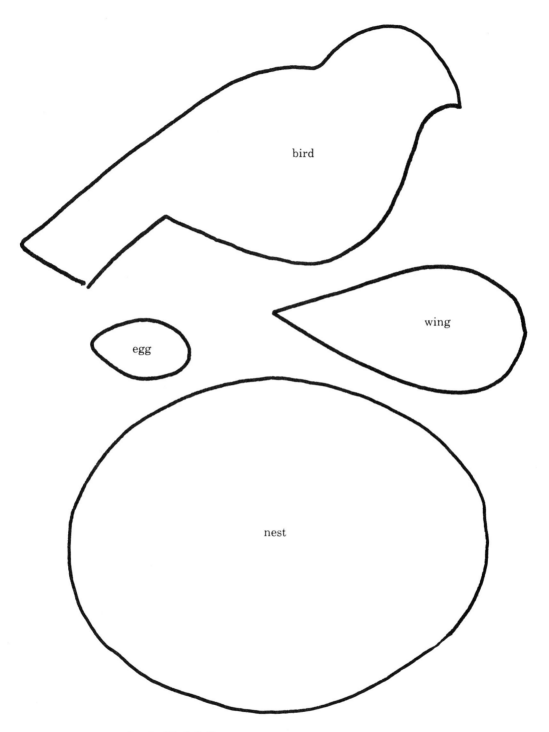

bird

wing

egg

nest

Fig. 3.31 Patterns for the Bird Collage.

might want to stitch in a few feathers on the gold wing as well, giving the bird an attractive, padded look. Stitch to the outside of the nest and sew that down freely. Then sew all around the outside edge of your picture. Cut off the stocking from the outside edges.

Add three gold lamé eggs under the bird. Over the edge of the nest, scatter half the thread pieces you've cut. Hold all this down by laying a piece of moss green bridal veiling over the picture and pinning it in place.

Again, with transparent thread and a free machine, sew around the eggs, around the outside of the bird and around the nest, managing to catch threads to anchor them. Yes, you will be sewing in a haphazard manner around the nest—and you do not have to sew every thread in place. With a very fine embroidery scissors, cut out the veiling from in front of the bird and the eggs.

String the small clay beads onto some of the remaining "nest" threads. Arrange the threads around the nest on top of those you have already sewn in place. Be very careful as you sew these threads in place; you don't want to hit beads with the darning foot. With transparent thread, sew above and below the beads to hold them in place (see Fig. 3.25).

An alternative method is to remove the darning foot. Press the fabric firmly against the needle plate as you sew down the threads. Be careful of your fingers. Thread up with a shiny brown rayon thread. With your machine set up for zigzag stitching, add texture and color to the nest by stitching a blob, lifting the presser foot lever and pulling the picture to stitch again in another spot. Cross and recross threads. I change colors several times (browns, beiges and greens). This also helps anchor the coarse threads.

The bird's eye can be added by sewing on a gold bead by hand, or with your machine, by building up a blob of thread. Your picture is complete. Pull off the freezer paper, or leave it in place. Cut off that extra margin from around your piece. Stretch the picture over a piece of batting and plywood and frame it. These pictures are so much fun to put together, and no two are alike.

Lesson 7. Smocking and gathering

Smocking

In hand smocking, fabric is gathered tightly into channels and embroidery is worked on top of the channels. Stitches chosen are open and stretchy.

Smocking by machine, on the other hand, will not be stretchy like hand smocking. After gathering with thread or cord, machine embroidery stitches usually hold the gathers in place. But if you use elastic, the gathering will stretch—but then, of course, you won't embroider over it.

There are at least a dozen ways to smock on your sewing machine, varying the method of gathering or embroidering, or varying the threads used. Here are several methods you can try. In each one, start with at least 2½ times the width needed for the finished pattern. For any garment, do the smocking first and then cut out the pattern.

Simple gathered smocking

First draw at least four lines across the 45"-wide (114.3cm-wide) fabric with a water-erasable marker. The lines should be about ½" (12.7mm) apart. Leave the seam allowances free of stitching. Anchor the threads, and then straight stitch along your drawn lines, leaving long ends of thread at the ends of the rows (Fig. 3.32A).

Stitch width: varies
Stitch length: varies
Needle position: center
Needle: #90
Feed dogs: up
Presser foot: open embroidery
Built-in stitch: zigzag or open embroidery type
Tension: *top*, normal; *bottom*, varies
Fabric: 2 or more 18″ × 45″ (45.7 × 114.3cm) pieces of medium-weight cotton; 1 yard (.9m) strip for gathering ruffles; several 12″ (30.5cm) or larger pieces of scrap fabrics
Threads: machine embroidery; monofilament
Accessories: water-erasable marker
Stabilizer: water-soluble, tear-away type

Pull on the bobbin threads to gather the fabric to 18″ (45.7cm) and knot every two threads together. Pin this to tear-away stabilizer.

Choose a decorative stitch and embroider across the fabric between the gathering lines of stitching (Fig. 3.32A). Then take out the gathering stitches and tear off the stabilizer.

Smocking with cordonnet

Use another piece of 18″ × 45″ (45.7 × 114.3cm) fabric. Thread the cordonnet through the throatplate or raised seam plate (Viking) of the machine. To gather, sew across the fabric, using a double needle (1.6mm) and pintuck or raised seam foot (Fig. 3.32B). Again, leave the seam allowances free of stitching. Use the presser foot as a width guide to sew at least three more rows. Stitch an even number of rows, at least four. Leave tails of cord at the beginning and end of each line.

Tie off pairs of the cords at the start. Pull the cords to gather the material to 18″ (45.7cm). Then tie a knot at the end of each. Remove the cordonnet from the machine.

Place a stabilizer under your work. Embroider over the cords and then remove the stabilizer.

Embroidering with thick thread in the bobbin

This may be used with either of the preceding methods for gathering. First complete the gathering. Turn the fabric over, topside down on the bed of the machine. Place water-soluble stabilizer under the gathers.

Stitch width: varies
Stitch length: varies
Built-in stitch: zigzag or open embroidery type
Needle position: center
Needle: #90
Feed dogs: up
Presser foot: open embroidery foot
Tension: *top,* normal; *bobbin,* varies with cord
Fabric: medium-weight cotton
Thread: monofilament or sewing thread for top; #5 or #8 pearl cotton for bobbin
Stabilizer: water-soluble

When you stitch up the samples, sew, look underneath to see if the pearl cotton is attached evenly and smoothly. Adjust tensions and stitch width as necessary.

Open built-in stitches look best—the simple zigzag is effective. Remove the stabilizer when your stitching is completed.

Smocking with elastic

Wind the bobbin with fine, round elastic. Do this by hand so it doesn't stretch. Again, stitch down rows ½″ (12.7mm) apart, gathering as you sew. The thread on top will show, so choose the color carefully. You can use this for bodices of sun dresses, nightgowns or swimsuits. This works best on delicate to lightweight fabrics.

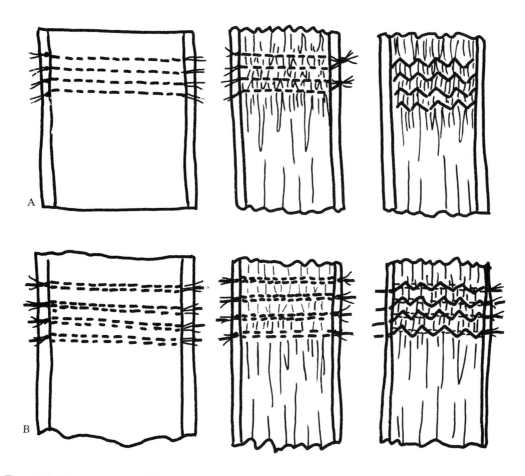

Fig. 3.32 Two ways to machine smock. A. Gather up rows of stitching and embroider between them. B. Gather the fabric, then using a cord and double needle, embroider over the gathers.

Another way to make fabric stretch, giving a shirred effect, is to use a round elastic through the hole of the throat plate or raised seam plate. Use regular thread on top and bobbin, and a zigzag setting that clears the elastic.

Alternately, stitch with a double needle and a straight stitch. Stitch several rows across the fabric using the presser foot as a guide, or draw the rows on the fabric with a water-erasable marker before stitching. Don't pull the elastic for gathering until all the stitching is completed. I use this meth-od at the top of children's knit skirts, as well as on waistlines of T-shirt dresses.

With 1/8" (3.2mm) flat elastic, use either the universal stitch or lycra stitch, width 4, length 2. If your machine does not have the lycra stitch (Fig. 3.33A), use the sewn-out zigzag, also called serpentine stitch (Fig. 3.33B). Thread the elastic through the opening in the braiding foot or use the groove in the open embroidery foot to guide it. On the Elna, use the elastic attachment accessory.

With the lycra or sewn-out zigzag set-

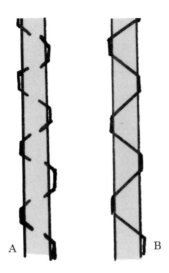

Fig. 3.33 Two ways to attach flat elastic. A. Lycra stitch. B. Universal stitch.

tings, the gathers can't be changed after they are sewn in, because the needle stitches into the elastic. Stretch the elastic while sewing. The more you stretch it, the more gathers it will create.

The universal stitch will sew on either side of the flat elastic and will not pierce it as the lycra stitch does. After stitching, adjust the gathers.

Gathering

Using cord

To gather light to heavyweight materials, use this, my all-time favorite method.

Stitch width: 2
Stitch length: 2
Needle position: center
Feed dogs: up

Zigzag over a cord, such as gimp or cordonnet. To keep the cord in position while stitching over it, use a cording foot. Place the cord in the hole and it will be fed through and covered perfectly (Fig. 3.34).

Pull up the cord to gather the fabric. Leave the cord in the fabric.

I use this for everything from skirts to dust ruffles to slipcovers. You won't break the gathering stitch as you often do when pulling on a basting thread. It saves hours.

Using elastic

Using the same settings as you did for cord, thread the elastic through the hole in the cording foot. Knot the elastic in back. Pull on it from the front while sewing a zigzag over it. I use this for quick sleeve finishes for little girls' dresses. If sewn about 1″ (2.5cm) from the finished edge, it creates a ruffle.

Using a gathering foot

Gathering yards of ruffles is easy with a gathering foot. It simultaneously gathers

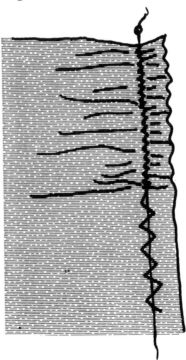

Fig. 3.34 Use an embroidery foot when zigzagging over cord to gather fabric.

and applies the gathers to another flat piece of fabric. The only drawback is that without seeing your fabric, I can't give you an iron-clad formula for how much fabric is needed to gather into, say, a 15" (39.1cm) ruffle.

The key to your estimates is to stitch a sample. Work with the same material you're going to use for the ruffle. Finer materials need to be gathered more fully than heavy fabrics do. Gathering depends upon fabric weight, tension and stitch length. The tighter the tension, the more gathering. The longer the stitch, the more fullness that can be locked into each stitch and the tighter the gathers—and the more

fabric you'll need. I admit I'm a coward and always add inches to be sure.

Even though this foot will gather a ruffle and apply it to fabric at the same time, I prefer gathering and attaching the gathers in two steps because of the difficulty in estimating the yardage I'll need for the ruffles. But, to do both steps at once, place the fabric to be attached to the ruffle in the slot of the gathering foot and the ruffle fabric under the foot. Keep the edges of both pieces of fabric even with the right side of the foot.

This does not exhaust the methods of gathering and smocking on the machine. Check your manuals for others.

Lesson 8. Pulling threads together

Satin stitching on top of loosely woven fabric builds up texture quickly by drawing the threads of the fabric together into ridges. Then you can connect the ridges for even more texture. As you can see in the sample (Fig. 3.35), this technique looks like lace.

If you're hesitant about stitching in open areas, place water-soluble stabilizer behind the fabric before stitching.

Stitch width: 0–4
Stitch length: 0
Needle position: center
Needle: #90
Feed dogs: lowered
Presser foot: darning foot
Tension: *top,* slightly loosened; *bobbin,* normal
Fabric: loosely woven cheesecloth type
Thread: machine embroidery, desired color top and bobbin
Accessories: spring hoop, water-soluble stabilizer (optional)

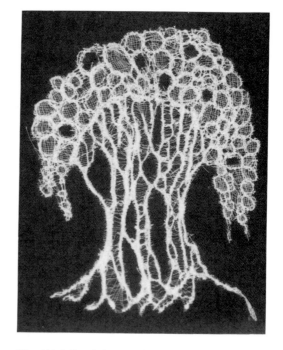

Fig. 3.35 Straight stitch and zigzag over loosely woven fabric produced both lacy and textured embroidery.

To learn this technique, stitch an imaginary tree of satin stitches and lacy straight stitches. It's not necessary to trace my design as this is done freely.

Put the fabric in a hoop. It must be stretched tightly. Bring the bobbin thread to the top and anchor the threads. Using the widest stitch setting, sew up and down in straight lines. At the down points, move the fabric over a bit and go up and down again. Continue until you have three or four rows of satin stitches. Then go back over them, zigzagging in between. This draws the previous lines together. Cut fabric threads if there is too much pulling and puckering.

Create branches on top and, when you come down to the bottom again, flare the line of stitching to resemble roots. Use the widest zigzags to stitch up and down again. Go back and zigzag over the whole tree again and again until the stitches are built up to your liking.

Change to a straight stitch and begin to stitch small circles at the top to crown the branches. Go from one to another. Cut or poke out the centers of some or all of the circles in the tree top, thus creating a lacy effect.

If you've used water-soluble stabilizer, then wash it out on completion of your work.

In the sample, I trimmed the tree from the background to show you the type of appliqué I add to my collages. It has a lacy look you can see through, which adds depth to the embroidery it's placed over. But sometimes I place the untrimmed appliqué over a background fabric and stitch it in place. After trimming it back to the stitches, I freely embroider over it with more satin stitches, with more ridges, building up more and more texture.

If you do a large enough square of threads pulled together with satin stitches, it can be used as a design for your tote bag. Or leave it untrimmed and still in the hoop for a window hanging.

CHAPTER 4

Adding Fabric to Fabric: Appliqué

- **Lesson 9. Methods of applying appliqués**
- **Lesson 10. Appliquéing with feed dogs up**
- **Lesson 11. Appliquéing with feed dogs lowered**

Once you know your machine as I know mine, you won't be satisfied stitching down all your appliqués with satin stitches. This chapter will show you several ways to place an appliqué onto a background successfully and teach a variety of methods for stitching it in place, including satin stitch, straight stitch, blind hem, and three-dimensional applications.

You'll make tote bag squares, Carrickmacross lace, and shadow work in these lessons. You will also work samples for your notebook to practice other appliqué methods.

Lesson 9. Methods of applying appliqués

Applying fabric to fabric takes two steps. Both are equally important. The first is to place the appliqué on the background in a way that keeps it in place, without puckering the fabric and with edges held down firmly, to enable you to do a perfect final stitching. The second step is the stitching. In Lessons 10 and 11, we'll try blind hems, straight stitching, blurring, scribbling and corded edges.

In appliqué, the best results are achieved when the applied and background fabrics have similar properties. For example, if using a cotton background fabric, it is best to use a similar weight appliqué fabric, and one that can be washed like the cotton. If washable, prepare the fabrics by washing and ironing them. They may be easier to work with if they are starched.

Match the grain lines of the appliqué to those of the background fabric. It's usually necessary to use a stabilizer under the fabric to prevent puckers when stitching. There are several methods for the first step. The first one wastes fabric, but the results are worth it.

Method A

Stretch both fabrics tightly in a hoop. I use a wooden hoop for this step because the fabric can be stretched and held more tightly than in a spring hoop. The fabric for the appliqué should be underneath–on the bed of the machine–with the topsides of both fabrics down. Draw the design on the wrong side of the base fabric, or place a paper pattern in the hoop, either pinning it there or catching it in the hoop with the fabric.

With the machine set up for free machining, single stitch around the design. Take the fabric out of the hoop, turn it over and cut the applied fabric back to the stitching line. Place the fabric back in the

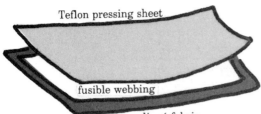

Teflon pressing sheet

fusible webbing

appliqué fabric

Fig. 4.1 To prepare an appliqué with fusible webbing, first place a piece of the fusible on the back of the appliqué fabric, cover it with the special Teflon sheet, and press in place.

hoop with the appliqué on top this time. Use one of the methods for final stitching discussed in Lessons 10 and 11.

Method B

For the next method, fusible webbing and a Teflon pressing sheet are needed. This will produce a slightly stiffer appliqué than the first method, but if done correctly, it will never produce a pucker.

Cut a piece of fabric and a piece of fusible webbing slightly larger than the appliqué (Fig. 4.1). With the fusible webbing on top of the appliqué fabric, place the Teflon sheet over it and iron until the fusible web-

bing melts (Fig. 4.2). When it cools, the Teflon can be peeled away. Cut out the appliqué from this piece of fabric and then iron it to the background fabric, using a Teflon sheet on top to protect your iron. Or use the paper-backed fusible webbing described in Chapter 1.

Method C

An alternative to fusible webbing is the appliqué paper backed with "glue." To use this paper, cut a piece of it and fabric approximately the size of the appliqué. Draw the design on the non-adhesive side of the paper, then iron the paper to the back of the fabric. After it adheres and cools, cut around the design and fabric, then peel the paper off the appliqué. The glue will have been transferred from the paper to the fabric. Iron the appliqué to the background.

If doing lettering or an appliqué where direction is important, then remember that this method gives you a flipped or mirror image of the original.

Method D

Plastic sandwich bags can also be used as a fusible—or try cleaners' garment bags.

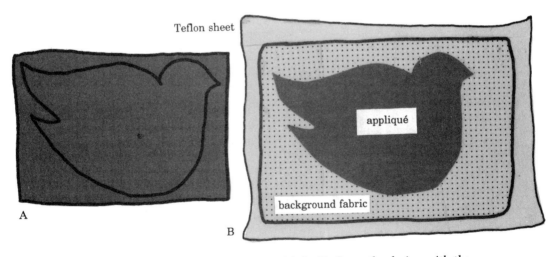

Teflon sheet

A

appliqué

background fabric

B

Fig. 4.2 A. Cut out the design from the appliqué fabric. B. Cover the design with the Teflon sheet again to press in place on the background fabric.

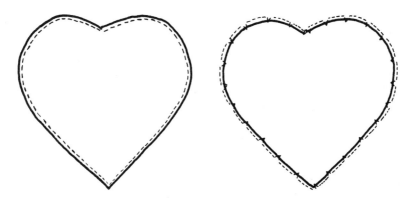

Fig. 4.3 To prepare and apply an appliqué for blind hemming, stitch all around it ¼" (6.3mm) from the edge (top). Fold under on the stitching, apply to the background and blind-hem-stitch in place (bottom).

Cut out a piece of plastic the size of the appliqué and place it between the backing fabric and appliqué.

Put brown wrapping paper over and under this "sandwich" so any plastic that is peeking out will be ironed onto the brown paper and not your iron or ironing board. Press it with an iron hot enough to melt the plastic and fuse the fabrics together.

Method E

If you wish to blind hem around the edge of an appliqué for step two, the appliqué must be prepared in another way (Fig. 4.3).

First, straight stitch around the appliqué on what will be the fold line. Cut the appliqué from the fabric, leaving a ¼" (6.3mm) seam allowance. Clip the edges and turn under on the stitched line. Trim off more seam allowance wherever fabric overlaps or creates bulk. Baste with stitches or a glue-stick. Press the edges flat. Baste in place on the background fabric–I

find it more accurate when done by hand. There is a wash-away basting thread on the market. If you use this it eliminates the need to pull out the basting later, and if it gets caught in your final stitching, there's no problem because it simply washes away. Now you can blind-hem the appliqué to the foundation.

If the appliqué is to be embroidered, it is sometimes best to do it first to prevent puckers in the background fabric. Embroidered patches can be appliquéd in many ways, the most common being satin stitching around the edge. But another way is to leave the edge almost devoid of stitching, cut out the appliqué and apply it with the same free stitches as the embroidery, to blend it into the background.

Even if fabric is to be heavily embroidered, embroider first on another piece of fabric, cut it out, and make it an appliqué. Use a glue stick or pin it in place. These appliqués are usually too thick to attach with fusible webbing.

Tote Bag Squares: (lower right, clockwise) Chapter 4, Lesson 10—Modified Reverse Applique, Edge-Stitch Applique, Straight Stitch Applique; Chapter 7, Lesson 19—Applique and Quilting

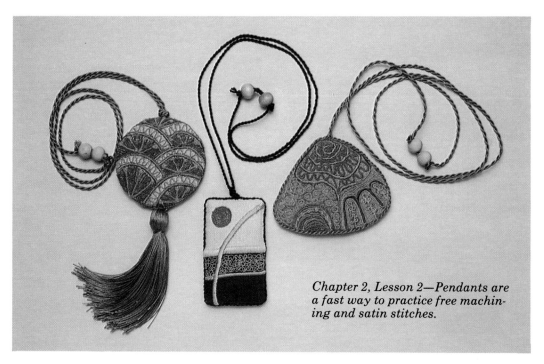

Chapter 2, Lesson 2—Pendants are a fast way to practice free machining and satin stitches.

Chapter 3, Lesson 5—Fringed Denim Rug

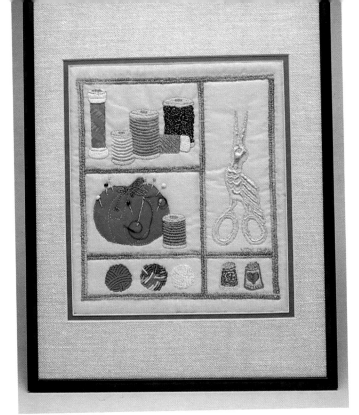

"Sewing Theme Shadow Box" by Yvonne Perez, San Diego, CA—thread on spools is satin stitch worked over upholstery needles.

Fish Outfit by Jean Van Koughnett, LaGrange, IL—Close-up of appliqued and stuffed fish jewelry (back of dress has fish appliques, dress has matching fish purse).

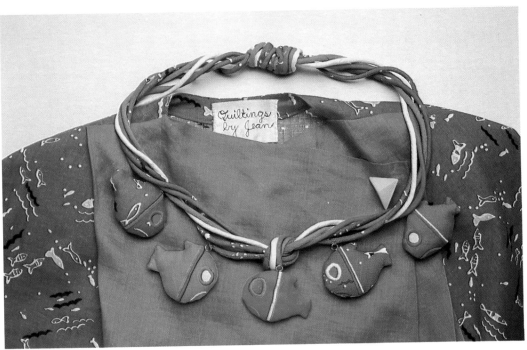

Appliqued Purse by Marion Spanjerdt, Toronto, Canada (collection of Marilyn Tisol)— Straight stitch applique.

Close-up of Polly, 17" doll by Edith Tanniru, DeWitt, NY—Machine-embroidered dress, crazy-quilted vest, hair attached by machine.

Lesson 10. Appliquéing with feed dogs up

Satin stitches three ways

In addition to keeping your machine in excellent condition, the perfect satin stitch is achieved by matching of fabric, needle, and thread. Always sew a sample, using the same fabric, needle and thread that will be used on the finished piece. Don't watch the needle, but keep your eyes on the line you'll be stitching. Check to see if the fabric is being fed through evenly. Open or close the length of the zigzags. Each machine has its own personality, so you must work this out for yours.

Standard method

Keep a few things in mind when attaching an appliqué with satin stitches: First, the stitch width should not overpower the appliqué. I almost always use a setting no wider than 2, along with an appliqué foot, because the satin stitches fit perfectly inside the groove on the underside of the foot. The groove guides my stitching so that satin stitches are perfect. If I use a wider stitch setting, then I use a foot with a wider groove–such as the open embroidery foot.

I prefer to cover the edge of an appliqué in two passes rather than one. Instead of a 1/2 length, start with 3/4. At the same time, dial the first pass slightly narrower than the final one. Instead of 4 width, dial down to 3 3/4 for the first pass.

Use a needle appropriate for the thread. The needle must be large enough to let the thread pass through freely and it must punch a large enough hole in the fabric to prevent the thread from fraying. For example, with rayon embroidery thread I use a #90 needle; on cotton embroidery thread, I use a #80 needle. On woven materials, I use a pierce-point needle instead of a universal point because I feel it gives me a more perfect edge. (The universal point is slightly rounded, so it deflects off the fibers and slips between them. When satin stitching on closely woven materials, this needle may create an uneven edge.)

Stained-glass method

Stained-glass is a type of satin-stitch appliqué in which your satin stitches are gray to black and extend out from the appliqué to the borders of the design. It is important to remember this, since not every design is appropriate for stained-glass.

Reverse appliqué

Reverse appliqué is the technique of layering from one to many fabrics on top of a background material. A design is straight-stitched through layers, then the fabric is cut away from portions of the design to reveal the fabric beneath. It is finished by satin stitching over the straight stitches. Reverse appliqué can be combined with appliqué from the top as well. To do a perfect reverse appliqué, put both fabrics in a hoop, topsides up, your appliqué fabric underneath. Draw the design on the top fabric or place the pattern on top of the fabrics in the hoop and straight stitch around the design. Remove the paper.

Stitch width: 2−4
Stitch length: 1/2 3/4 or adjust for your machine
Needle position: center
Presser foot: appliqué foot or open embroidery foot
Feed dogs: up
Tension: *top*, slightly loosened; *bobbin*, normal

Take the fabrics out of the hoop and cut out the top fabric inside the design area. Put the fabric back in the hoop, slip stabilizer between hoop and machine, and then satin stitch the edges. When finished, you may want to cut away the extra appliqué fabric on the back to eliminate bulk.

This method often affords better control of the appliqué when applying small pieces to a design.

Project
Tote Bag Square
(Modified Reverse
Appliqué)

This square, shown in Fig. 4.4, could be reverse appliqué. In fact, I began it that way, but found that there were too many layers, so much bulk to sew through that the satin stitches didn't meet my standards. I faked reverse appliqué by using the following layering technique and cut out as much fabric underneath as I could

Also, I have my reasons for not cutting

Stitch width: 1 1/2 – 2 1/2
Stitch length: satin stitch
Needle position: center
Needle: #90 sharp
Feed dogs: up
Presser foot: appliqué or embroidery
Tension: *top,* slightly loosened; *bobbin,* normal
Fabric suggestions: lightweight cotton, 9″ squares of orange, yellow, purple, green
Thread: orange machine embroidery
Accessories: fusible webbing, Teflon pressing sheet, dressmaker's carbon, empty ballpoint pen, tracing paper
Stabilizer: Iron-on freezer paper

out each piece and then fitting it all together like a jigsaw puzzle. It takes too much time trying to get them to fit perfectly—they never do—so I'd rather not use that method.

Transfer the design in Fig. 4.4 onto tracing paper. Use dressmaker's carbon between the design and the purple background fabric. Then, with the ballpoint pen, transfer the design to the purple fabric. This is your guide.

Next, cut apart the design on the tracing paper. Using the pieces of the design, cut out fabrics for the shapes, each larger than the finished size. With fabric topside on the ironing board, place Stitch Witchery over the fabric and a Teflon pressing sheet over that. Press to adhere Stitch Witchery to the underside of the fabric. Cut out the design in this manner: Only the yellow center piece will be cut out exactly. Place it on the purple background. Each of the other pieces will be cut slightly larger on one side, but exactly on the drawn line on the other side (i.e., to the right, the green leaf will be cut with ¼″ (6.3mm) seam allowance on the left side and slipped under the yellow center. The orange piece, which is next, will be cut out with ¼″ (6.3mm) seam allowance on the left side and slipped under the green leaf. The yellow patch will be cut out with ¼″ (6.3mm) seam allowance on the curve and slipped under the orange piece.

On the left side of the yellow center, all the seam allowances will be on the righthand side. Before you press in place, be sure that there are no seam allowances peeking out where they don't belong.

I prefer lifting off all the layers and then, beginning with the first layer, place and press, go on to the second layer and so on. The pieces will adhere better.

Cutting and placing the appliqués in this way allows you to stitch on only one raw edge; it also eliminates the bulk of layering each piece and then cutting down to the colors beneath.

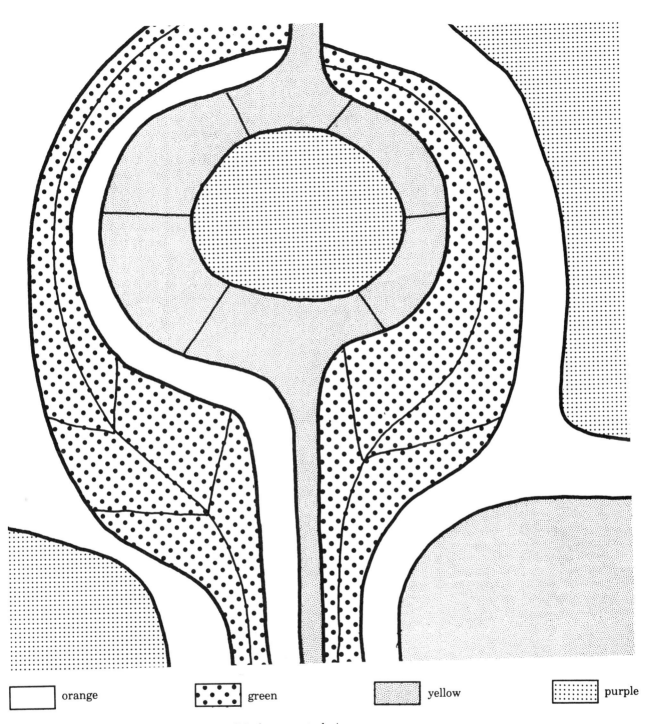

| | orange | | green | | yellow | | purple |

Fig. 4.4 Flower appliqué tote square; modified reverse technique.

Iron freezer paper to the back before you begin stitching.

This design can be easily stitched because most of the curves are gradual, with few sharp corners. Using orange thread, I began by stitching short lines through the yellow fabric and veins in the leaves to give my appliqué a stained-glass look. The first pass will be short lines and veins set at stitch width 1 1/2 and the appliqué edges at stitch width 2. Keep the satin stitches slightly open on the first pass. On the second pass, use a slightly wider 2 width for the short lines and veins and 2 1/2 width for the satin stitches. Use a stitch length that will produce a close, smooth satin stitch.

Sew at a moderate speed. When your stitches begin to slant at curves and corners, stop with needle down. Lift the presser foot and turn the fabric, stitch one or two stitches or whatever it takes to keep the satin stitches straight. Continue stitching, remembering to always turn with the needle in the fabric. Finish the square as described in Chapter 12.

Blind hemming

A second way to attach appliqués to a background is with the blind hemstitch. Use the edging foot or blind-stitch foot. Prepare the appliqué according to Method E (see Fig. 4.3) and use monofilament thread on the top. Use your machine's blind-hem built-in stitch; length and width are determined by you, but start with a stitch width 1 and a stitch length 2. Stitch around the appliqué, letting the straight stitches fall just outside the appliqué, with the bite of the widest stitch catching the edge. You can set up the machine to give the look you want. Do you want a wide bite? Then set the width to a higher number. The length of the stitch determines the closeness of those two stitches that go up and back, holding the appliqué in place. Find the right length by doing a sample.

Use this method to attach patch pockets and to couch down heavy threads and cords. Usually monofilament is used on the top because it is almost invisible.

If you change the monofilament to a thread that will contrast with the fabric, this stitch gives the look of buttonholing by hand.

A line of blind hemstitching is used in the greeting card project in Lesson 4 (Fig. 3.9).

Straight stitching

To apply fabric with a straight edge-stitch, you will place the appliqué on the background as you did for blind hemming (if you are working with non-wovens like suedes or felt, don't press the edges under). Use an edging, zipper, or blind-stitch foot. Set the straight stitch at a 2 length and stitch width at 0.

With the presser foot in place on the fabric, set the needle position to slightly within the appliqué. Stitch around the motif.

Project
Tote Bag Square (Edge-Stitch Appliqué)

This tote bag square (Fig. 4.5) uses straight stitching on felt. Because there are several layers of felt used, it gives the appearance of a quilted flower.

Press fusible webbing behind each piece of felt, except chartreuse. That will be the background onto which you will appliqué the other fabrics. Within the 9" chartreuse square, draw a square 6¾".

Transfer the design in Fig. 4.5 to tracing paper. Cut apart and place the patterns on the felt pieces. Cut out petals, leaves and stamens (Fig. 4.6). Cut five strips, each 9" × ¼", from the dark green felt.

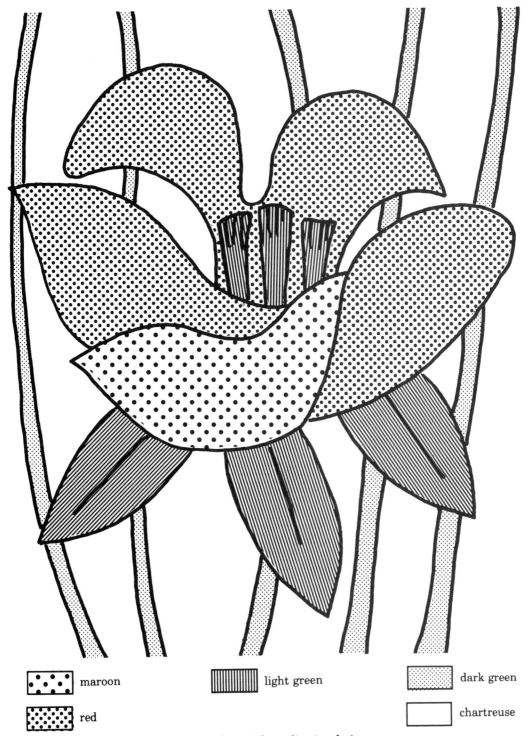

| | maroon | | light green | | dark green |
| | red | | | | chartreuse |

Fig. 4.5 Design for tote bag square, edge-stitch appliqué technique.

Fig. 4.6 Edge-stitch appliqué pattern pieces.

Arrange your design within the 6¾″ square. First place the five strips on the background. Next, press and stitch down the center of each with monofilament thread.

On top of this, arrange the Christmas red petals and slip the ends of the three light-green stamens underneath as shown. Slip one light-green leaf under the petal at right before you press and stitch all the pieces in place. Stitch as closely as you can to the edge of the petals, but when stitching the three stamens, sew a straight line down the center of each one. Fringe them by clipping the tops as shown. To attach the leaf, stitch around the edge and then part way down through the center.

Place the maroon petal on top and arrange the two remaining leaves underneath it as indicated. Stitch around them and part way down through the centers of the leaves. This achieved the effect I wanted, but you may prefer to stitch the leaf centers down entirely, and add vein lines, too.

Finish the square as described in Chapter 12.

Project
Tote Bag Square
(Straight Stitch)

The next sample also uses straight stitches to hold appliqués in place, but is otherwise quite different. I used turquoise and purple fabric plus all the tote bag colors on this one and layered several of the designs. The background is yellow.

Apply fusible webbing to all fabrics except the yellow background square, using the Teflon pressing sheet. Trace the appliqués from Fig. 4.7. Complete the large circle, even though it is partially covered by other pieces. The streak of lightning is in two parts. Add seam allowance to the righthand side of the smallest point (and slip the appliqué under the circle later). Cut out each appliqué, using the pattern as your guide, and apply to the background fabric using Method B for fusible webbing.

With the water-erasable marker, draw lines from top to bottom every ½″ (12.7mm) across the square. Starting at

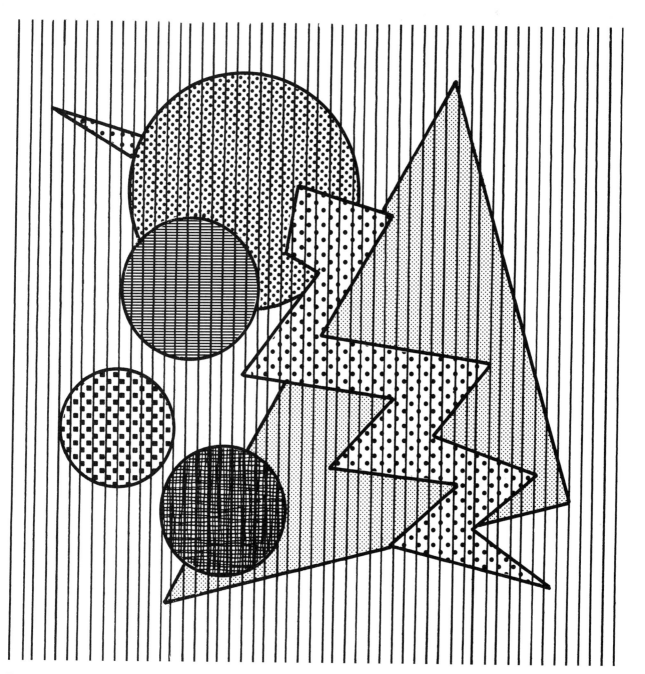

Fig. 4.7 Pattern for tote square. Use the fusible webbing method to attach geometric shapes to the background fabric, then stitch evenly spaced lines of straight stitching to hold them.

the top right corner, straight stitch to the bottom on the first line. Turn and stitch back, bottom to top, on the next line. Continue across the square.

Go back and stitch between those lines. You may be able to use the side of your presser foot as a measuring guide. Make one last pass and stitch between the lines again. There are now straight-stitch lines from top to bottom every ⅛″ (3.2mm).

Instead of row after row of straight stitches to hold appliqués in place, try satin stitches or use a double needle. Also try couching down metallics and thick cords. Finish the squares as described in Chapter 12.

Cording edges

Corded edges give appliqués and decorative patches a neat, exact finish. Use a cording foot if cord is fine enough to be threaded through it. You may also try an appliqué, open embroidery, pintuck, or hemmer (with zigzag opening) to guide cord.

When finishing patches, sew the corded edges in two passes. Place the patch over typing paper or tear-away stabilizer. You'll need two pieces–one for each pass–and they must be large enough to extend past the edge of the patch.

On the first pass, apply the cord, sewing at a narrower stitch width, and with stitch length slightly longer than the final pass.

The final stitching is done with a close satin stitch, the needle stitching down in the fabric on one side of the cord, but stitching off the cord and fabric on the other side. Leave enough cord at the beginning and end to poke to the back and work into the stitches. Use a needle with a large eye to do this by hand. Or, when you reach the end of the first pass, cut the cord to slightly overlap the start. If you can cut it on an angle, the join will not be noticeable when the second pass is completed.

It is not necessary to cover the entire cord if the cord itself is decorative or is a color that adds to the effect you wish to achieve. When I had to appliqué dozens of velveteen crosses to a woolen ecclesiastical garment, I used a velour cord and an open zigzag, and sewed with a thread the color of the velour. When finished, the velour edges looked like an extension of the velveteen.

Lesson 11. Appliquéing with feed dogs lowered

In this lesson, the appliqués are sewn in place freely; sometimes edges are not completely covered.

Set up your machine by lowering the feed dogs, using either a hoop or ironed-on freezer paper, and loosening the top tension slightly.

Blurring

What is blurring? Apply a fabric to another by starting to stitch within the appliqué. Then, following the shape of the appliqué, stitch around and around it, extending the stitching out into the background fabric. It's difficult to tell where one begins and the other leaves off. That is called blurring.

Although the sample here uses transparent fabrics, blurring can be done with any type of fabric. I chose to combine blurring with sheers and overlays to show you how to create pictures that look like watercolors. Thread color is usually the same as the appliqué, but never limit yourself. Use other colors as well.

When working with transparent fabrics, use pins to hold the appliqués in place. If possible, hold both in a hoop while sewing.

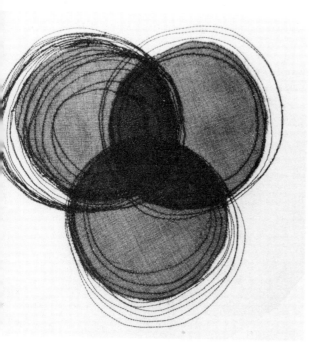

Fig. 4.8 Blurring the edges of appliqués.

Project
Flower of Sheers and Overlays

Use this floral piece as a pillow top or slip it into your notebook. To do the flower sample (Fig. 4.9), set up the machine.

Use the circle and leaf shape to make the patterns. Cut out several dozen 1″ (2.5cm) circles in pink transparent fabric. Also cut the same number of 2″ (5.1cm) long leaf shapes from green transparent fabric. Patterns are provided in Fig. 4.10. You may not use all of these petals and leaves: It will depend upon how much they are overlapped and how large an area you're covering with the design.

Arrange and overlap the leaves in a circle on the background fabric, points toward the center. Plan so they will fit within the hoop, keeping the leaves at least an inch (2.5cm) inside. If the presser foot gets

Attach one layer at a time, sewing a straight stitch around the appliqué and then cutting back to the stitching. Blur the edges. Then stretch the next transparent fabric in the hoop, stitch and cut away excess, then blur the edges.

To blur edges, find any point inside the appliqué. Stitch round and round, in ever-widening circles, until the edge of the appliqué is reached. But don't stop. Keep stitching past the edge and into the background. Three transparent circles applied in this way, one overlapping the next, the third overlapping the others, makes a good sample (Fig. 4.8). Possibilities will grow from this one idea: try many colors, overlapping them to make other colors; give depth to a picture by overlapping so that the color becomes more intense as the layers are built up, and recedes where only one layer is used.

Stitch width: 0 — widest
Stitch length: 0
Needle position: center
Needle: #80
Feed dogs: lowered
Presser foot: darning foot
Tension: *top,* slightly loosened; *bobbin,* normal
Fabric suggestion: 10″ (25.4cm) square medium-weight white fabric for the background; ¼ yard (22.9cm) green transparent fabric; ⅛ yard (11.4cm) pink transparent fabric; 12″ (30.5cm) square off-white bridal veiling
Threads: machine embroidery in yellow, green, and pink
Accessories: 7″ (17.8cm) spring hoop
Stabilizer: tear-away

Fig. 4.9 Use bridal veiling to hold small pieces of appliqué fabric in place.

too close to the edge, it will be difficult to sew around the appliqués without hitting the darning foot on the hoop.

Lay down the circles of color for the flower head, starting in the middle of the leaves. New colors pop out for the leaves and petals as you overlap, arrange and rearrange. Leave the center of the flower open. Don't pin down any of these small pieces.

After completing the arrangement of the sheers and overlays, cover with the piece of bridal veil to help hold them all in place. Pin the veiling down in several places near the center of the flower and at the edges of the fabric. Lift this carefully from the table and place it in a hoop. Slip stabilizer under it.

Start by sewing around the petals of the flower. Use pink thread on the top, green thread on the bobbin. Stitch the petals very freely. Bring the stitching out past them, or inside, or make stitched circles between them. Stitch circles within circles.

Then change the top thread to green. Stitch around the leaves in the same free-flowing way. Go up the centers and down, stitching in veins on some and leaving others without.

Now only the center is left to stitch. Change the top thread to yellow and set stitch width to the widest zigzag, stitch length 0, needle position to the left. Anchor your threads in the center of the flower. Stitch in the same spot at least a dozen times to build up a nubby "seed" (see Fig. 3.2). Anchor the threads again. Lift the presser foot and move to another place. Do another seed. There's no need to clip threads until all the seeds are completed. Keep building up the nubs and moving your needle from one place to the next until the flower center is to your liking. Then clip the threads between the zigzag areas.

Change the top thread back to green. Set stitch width back to 0, needle position center. Sew around the seeds. Go from one to another until all are outlined. When the picture is complete, take it out of the hoop. Most of the stabilizer will drop away; the rest can be pulled off (or left on, since it won't show).

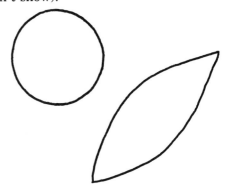

Fig. 4.10 Patterns for the flower design.

The bridal veil can be left as is. However, I often clip out areas to create color changes.

Scribbling

Scribbling is like darning over appliqués, but you will use both straight and zigzag stitches. It's a good way to lay in big areas of color without having to cover the areas with heavy embroidery.

The appliqué picture in Fig. 4.11 was placed on the outside of a tote bag. Use the patterns in Fig. 4.12 as a guide, enlarging or reducing to fit your purpose.

Stitch width: varies
Stitch length: 0
Needle position: center
Needle: #90
Feed dogs: lowered
Presser foot: darning foot
Tension: *top,* slightly loosened; *bobbin,* normal
Fabric suggestion: medium-weight cotton
Thread: machine embroidery on top; sewing or darning thread on bobbin
Accessories: glue stick
Stabilizer: ironed-on freezer paper

Apply the appliqués with a dab of glue stick and begin to stitch the edges down freely with either a straight or a zigzag stitch. Sew freely over the entire appliqué first to anchor it before embroidering the designs. Stitch inside and over the edges of the appliqués. If you can live with raw edges, then don't be too particular about covering them exactly. Here is a good place to blur edges. Add to the design by laying in different colors with the same free machining. Add as much stitching as you wish, but don't cover the entire appliqué, as that would defeat the purpose. Let most of the color show through. It's like sketching with colored pencils.

Stitching Carrickmacross

Carrickmacross is an Irish lace made with appliqués of batiste. Tiny pops, or eyelets, are embroidered in the fine hexagonal net which is used as the ground, and it has a picot edge. If hand done, this type of lace is very fragile, but our machine version is both beautiful and sturdy (Fig. 4.13).

Fig. 4.11 This is part of a design that has been appliquéd to a tote bag, using free-machining to hold the appliqués in place.

Fig. 4.12 Use these patterns to create one element of the design shown in Fig. 4.11.

Project
Carrickmacross Doily

Instead of batiste, we'll use organdy. I've used a polyester for the veiling, so my fabric will be the same. It will be white on white, typical of Carrickmacross lace.

Copy the design in Fig. 4.14 onto the organdy, using a water-erasable pen. Slip the net underneath the organdy and put them both into a spring hoop. If possible, always use a hoop large enough so you can do the entire design without having to move the fabric and net.

Set up your machine for free embroidery. Anchor threads and stitch on the

67

Stitch width: 0
Stitch length: 0
Needle position: center
Needle: #80
Feed dogs: lowered
Presser foot: darning foot
Tension: *top,* slightly loosened; *bobbin,* normal
Fabric suggestion: white polyester organdy; fine white polyester hexagonal veiling
Thread: white cotton machine embroidery thread and white cordonnet (optional)
Accessories: 7″ (17.8cm) spring hoop; water-erasable pen
Stabilizer: water-soluble

those tiny spots. Then go back and poke holes in the centers with a darning needle. Set the stitch width to 2, and slowly (use the moderate speed setting on your machine if available), almost hand-walk the stitching from center to outside with the zigzag. Stitch twice, turn the hoop a hair, stitch 2 more times, turn the hoop, stitch again, all around the pop.

Hand-worked Carrickmacross lace has a cord couched down around the appliqués to hold them in place. To do this by machine, stitch around the appliqués only once before cutting back. Do not trim around the outside edge. Put the piece back in the hoop upside down. Use cordonnet or pearl cotton in the bobbin.

Before beginning to outline the appliqués, dip the needle down and bring the

lines around each motif at least three times. It may be necessary to stitch a fourth pass on some, but make it look consistent: Don't leave some lines with one pass, others with four. Plot the course of the needle ahead of time so there won't be too many stops and starts.

When the design is finished, take it out of the hoop and cut out all the areas that are to be free of organdy. Use sharp, fine-pointed scissors. It helps to lift areas away from the net with the point of a seam ripper and then clip.

Should you cut the net, don't panic. Put it back under the needle and stitch a few lines of straight stitching over the cut, blending it into the other stitches already there. It will look like it was meant to be there all the time.

When that is completed and looks great, decide whether to go on or to stop while you're ahead. You may go one step further, as real Carrickmacross lace always has a picot edge and small eyelets in the net, as shown in Fig. 4.15.

To stitch the eyelets, mark some places, such as the middles of the flowers, that you think need pops. Stitch freely around

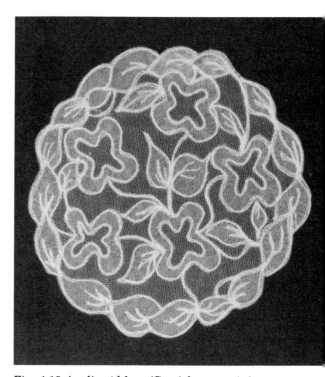

Fig. 4.13 Appliquéd lace (Carrickmacross), is made quickly using organdy and fine hexagonal net.

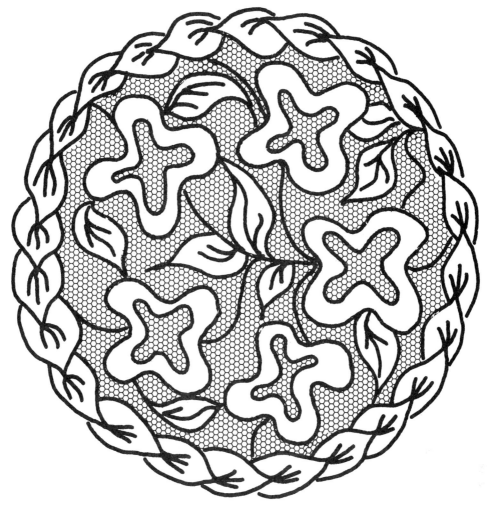

Fig. 4.14 The pattern for appliquéd lace.

cord up to the top. Hold both threads to one side as you take several stitches along the design. In other words, don't anchor the cord, as is usually done with thread. Later go back and work the threads into the stitches on the backside of the design.

Picots around the edge should be left until the rest of the stitching is completed.

Cut back to the edge. Use two layers of

Fig. 4.15 Eyelets and picots in Carrickmacross.

69

water-soluble stabilizer. The topside of the appliqué should be pinned against the stabilizer. Put all this into the hoop. First stitch the cord around the leaves at the inside edge. Then, with a water-erasable pen, mark small dots every ⅛" (3.2mm) along the edge to use as a guide for the picots. Stitch in by following the edge and making small loops at each mark. Take it out of the hoop and wash the stabilizer and blue pen marks out of the fabric.

What we've made is a small doily but, if you're like me, you are not big on small doilies. This is a fast technique, so think big. Try it for the edge of a bridal veil or for the bodice and puffed sleeves of the wedding dress itself. Now that's what I call a long-cut, but definitely worth it.

Layering transparent fabrics

Shadow work is my favorite. I love the painterly effects of combining colors and toning down with whites. It's done using sheers and overlays. In the picture made in the following project, the color does not come from a colored cotton fabric layered between organdies; instead, these flowers are created only from transparent fabrics.

Project Shadow Work Picture

In this project, I switch from feed dogs up to feed dogs lowered or covered, but most of the stitching is done freely, so I've put it in this lesson. This design (Fig. 4.16) will give you an idea of what can be done with only white, mauve and green organza.

Place the white organza over the design (Fig. 4.17) and trace it off with a water-erasable marker. Layer two mauves behind each flower on the white organza and pin them in place. Put this in a hoop.

With the machine set for free machin-

Stitch width: 0 – 4
Stitch length: 0 – 1/2
Needle position: center
Needle: #70
Feed dogs: up, lowered
Presser foot: appliqué, open embroidery, or darning foot
Tension: *top*, slightly loosened; *bobbin*, normal
Fabric: white, mauve, and green organza
Thread: green machine embroidery
Accessories: spring hoop; water-erasable marker
Stabilizer: water-soluble

Fig. 4.16 Layers of transparent fabrics give a painterly effect to shadow work.

70

Fig. 4.17 Shadow work design.

ing, without anchoring the threads, straight stitch around the flowers twice. Lift the needle and go to the flower centers. Stitch twice around each center, also: The lines should be next to each other, not on top of each other. Cut back to the stitching around the outside edge, but not too close.

Place the green organza behind the leaf areas and stitch in place with two lines of stitching. Cut back to the stitching at the edges.

Set up your machine for normal sewing. Put feed dogs up and use the appliqué foot. Use stitch width 2, stitch length 1/2 or a setting that will produce a smooth satin stitch. Sew around the flowers and leaves. Be careful: sew too closely and the stitches will cut the fabric.

From the front of your picture, cut the white organza from one flower, the white and one mauve layer from another. Turn the hoop over. Cut out one layer of mauve from the back on another. Or from the back, cut out both layers of color, leaving only the white organdy and the flower center intact. Can you imagine the combinations and shades of mauve you can create?

The large leaf is divided into four sections. In the first section, cut out the top white layer and place a layer of green behind the remaining green layer to darken it. In the second area, cut out the white and leave just green. In the third, place white behind the section to make it three layers. The fourth is left as is, the white in front of the green.

Once you have finished the flowers and leaves, go back to the flower centers and blur them out by stitching spirals from the centers out to the edges. Or start at the edges and travel to the outside of the flowers. Leave some flowers with only the first stitching around the center.

Satin stitches should be sewn through at least two layers of fabric. Ordinarily, we'd add stabilizer, but tear-away could leave specks in the fabric that might show

through. To prevent this, use green organza as a backing for the stems. The lines are satin stitched, then the stabilizing organza is cut back to the stitching.

Finish up with straight stitching. Set up again for free machining. Using water-soluble stabilizer behind the fabric, set the machine on stitch width 0, stitch length 0, to sew in the accent lines.

If one of the fabrics has pulled away from the satin stitches, don't give up. Layer a piece of transparent fabric underneath and stitch it on. Then cut away the original one. Or put a piece of organza underneath, use straight stitching or zigzags to sew in some lines, and pretend you wanted it that way. On the flowers, too: If by mistake you cut through two layers instead of one, leave it or layer something behind it. Sometimes blurring out more lines of stitching will attach and hide any mistakes.

Keep the stitching light and airy, with no wide satin stitches. There should be more fabric showing than stitching. When finished, wash out the stabilizer and pen marks.

This type of shadow work is quite fragile and I suggest using it for pictures or window hangings, rather than for clothing.

Project
Stitching Three-Dimensional Appliqués

One of the prettiest dresses I've ever seen was at a fraternity dance back when we thought we had to wear yards of tulle and gobs of ruffles. This dress was a beautiful white organdy exception. Over the entire skirt were scattered lavender and peach pansy appliqués of organdy. They were attached only at the centers. It was a

Stitch width: 0
Stitch length: 0
Needle position: center
Needle: #60 or #70
Feed dogs: lowered
Presser foot: darning foot or no presser foot, tailor-tacking foot (optional)
Tension: *top,* loosened; *bobbin*, normal
Fabric suggestion: mauve and green organdy
Thread: machine embroidery thread to match
Accessories: spring hoop; water-erasable marker
Stabilizer: water-soluble type

plain dress except for this scattering of flowers.

Detached appliqués do not have to have a heavy satin stitch edge, and I think you'll agree that straight stitching on fine fabric is easier and more beautiful. After all, that was a long time ago and I've never forgotten that dress.

Place a layer of water-soluble stabilizer between two layers of mauve organdy. Clip this into the spring hoop. Draw the design in Fig. 4.18 on it with a water-erasable marker. You will copy the petal design twice. The small sample is done in pieces and combined later (Fig. 4.19).

Set the machine on moderate speed for accuracy. Stitch three times around the edges with a straight stitch. Lines should

Fig. 4.18 Three-dimensional appliqué design.

Fig. 4.19 Pattern pieces for floral 3-D appliqué.

be close together but not on top of each other. Use a colored thread that matches or is a shade darker than the fabric. Cut out the petals close to the stitching, but not too close.

The leaves should be worked in the same way on green organdy. Stitch only straight stitches as you follow the pattern. Go into the centers and stitch the veins as well. Cut out the leaves.

Place the flower petals on top of each other—stagger them so the petals underneath are not hidden by the top layer. Place this over the leaves and stitch them together with mauve thread by following the stitching in the center of the petals. You may go a step further and fringe the center. Using the tailor tacking foot, green thread, stitch width 2 and stitch length almost 0, stitch in several places in the center of the flower. Finish by holding the flower under the faucet and rinsing out some, but not all, of the stabilizer. Shape the flower and leaves carefully and let them dry. They will be stiff, as if heavily starched, and will retain their shapes. How can you use these three-dimension appliqués? Add a band of them to a bodice of

74

Carrickmacross lace. Make an utterly fake corsage or a flowered hat. Add the flower to a cord for a necklace.

Helpful Hints for Appliqué

If an appliqué bubbles, fix it by taking it out of the hoop and nicking the base fabric beneath the appliqué, which will then allow the base to lay flat.

Or slit the back a bit and fill the appliqué area with cotton. This is called trapunto. Hand whip the slit closed. Machine stitch on top of the appliqué to add to the design and hold the batting in place.

Another way to keep appliqué puckers from showing is to hide them by hand or machine embroidering over the appliqué.

When layering net, there is sometimes a moiré look to it that spoils the effect of your picture. To eliminate it, change the direction of one of the layers.

Don't limit yourself to fabric appliqués; thread appliqués are also effective. Work spider webs in another fabric, cut them out, and apply.

Work lace in space inside a small ring. Apply it to a background by free machining all around the inside edge of the ring. Then cut the ring from the lace.

Check out Lesson 6 on beads, baubles, and shishas.

Do pulled and drawn threads with the machine on one fabric and attach them to another background.

CHAPTER 5

Stitching Across Open Spaces

- **Lesson 12. Cutwork and eyelets**
- **Lesson 13. Free-machined needlelace**
- **Lesson 14. Battenberg lace**
- **Lesson 15. Hemstitching**
- **Lesson 16. Stitching in rings**
- **Lesson 17. Making Alençon lace**

People have been stitching in space for a hundred years; you can, too. However, if you are nervous about doing it, stitching on water-soluble stabilizer usually produces the same effects with even better results. Water-soluble stabilizer is so thin and pliable that placing multiple layers of it in a hoop, along with fabric, is no problem. Another reason I am sold on it is that, once the design is drawn on the stabilizer, it can be stitched exactly, as if stitching on fabric. That isn't possible when actually stitching in space. I use it for cutwork because it holds the cut edges in place while I stitch them and sometimes I use it on both sides of the fabric to give it even more stability.

I use stabilizer when stitching in rings, too. It keeps threads in place until they are anchored. There is no problem with slipping, as often happens when stitching in space. Practice on water-soluble stabilizer, but if your machine is capable of it, graduate to open space and try that. There are occasions for both techniques.

This chapter includes cutwork, stitching in rings, creating needlelace, and stitching both Battenberg and Alençon laces. Hemstitching is included, as well. Be sure to keep all your samples in your notebook. You may not use an idea today or tomorrow, but maybe next year you'll refer back to your notebook and find just what you're looking for to make a special gift, or welcome a new baby. My notebook is especially valuable when I want to find machine settings for a technique I haven't used in weeks. No matter how well you know your machine, you can't remember every detail of a method you've tried.

Lesson 12. Cutwork and eyelets

Cutwork

Cutwork is the forerunner of all needlemade laces. It was common as early as the sixteenth century. In handmade cutwork, part of the background fabric is cut away and threads are stretched from one side of the open area to the other. Bars of buttonhole stitches are worked over the stretched threads and the cut edges. Cutwork can be done on most sewing machines, using satin stitches in place of buttonhole stitches.

Project Cutwork Needlecase

When I wanted to do a cutwork project on the machine without dedicating my life to a large, time-consuming sailor collar or tablecloth, I found that the needlecase in Fig. 5.1 was exactly the right size. The single design can be used as a repeat pattern and it can be combined with embroidery, appliqué or shadow work.

I traced the pattern (Fig. 5.2) on paper two different times. On one pattern I added lines where I wanted the thread bars, called "brides," to be.

Before you begin this or any project, practice, using the same fabric, needle and threads, stitch settings and stabilizers you will use on your finished piece. For this design, I practiced turning corners and satin stitching curves, as well as filling spaces with thread bars.

Cutwork is not usually backed by any-

Stitch width: 0 – 2
Stitch length: 0 to satin stitch
Needle position: center
Needle: #80
Feed dogs: up, lowered or covered
Presser foot: darning foot, open embroidery foot
Tension: *top*, slightly loosened; *bobbin*, normal
Fabric suggestion: closely woven linen or kettlecloth
Thread: machine embroidery
Accessories: spring hoop; tracing paper; small, sharp embroidery scissors; pencil, water-erasable marker, and permanent white marker
Stabilizer: water-soluble

thing, but on this needlecase you can see that it is a necessity.

Place the pattern without the thread bars on the back of the fabric and slip them both into a hoop. The topside of the fabric will be against the machine. Lower or cover the feed dogs and take the presser foot off. Straight stitch around the outlines of the design two times with the same thread you'll use for the satin stitching. (Do not stitch the bars at this time.)

Take the fabric out of the hoop and peel off the pattern. Cut out the larger area. Put a piece of stabilizer over the topside and one underneath the fabric, and place all three layers in the hoop. Slip the second pattern under the hoop. With a permanent

Fig. 5.1 The cutwork design on this needlecase can be used once, or as a repeat pattern.

Fig. 5.2 Cutwork pattern to copy.

white marker, trace the bars on the top stabilizer. Put the pattern aside until later.

With stitch width set to 0, freely stitch in the bars. Do the long, middle branching line first. Anchor the thread at the top by sewing in one place a few stitches, make a pass from top to bottom and then back again. As you sew from the bottom on that second pass, stitch the branches out and back as well.

Go back to stitch width 1 1/2. Stitch the first pass from top to bottom, moving the hoop quite quickly (remember the branches). Then, stitch back up from the bottom: This time move your hoop slowly. The stitches will be closer together. Remember, you control this by how fast you move the hoop. The stitches will look like

satin stitches in space. Anchor each branch by sewing at 0 width into the fabric just beyond the stay-stitching. Zigzag to the top and anchor the thread.

Stitch the short bars at each side next. Anchor the threads at the top of the first bar, just beyond the two rows of straight stitching. Sew straight stitches across to the other side, anchor the threads again, and come back on the same line. Then begin zigzagging back across these threads with a 1 1/2 stitch width. When you reach the other side, stop, turn the width to 0 and follow the stay-stitch line to the next bar position. Sew across, back, and then zigzag as you did the first one. Complete all the brides on each side.

Cut out all three smaller shapes that are

left in the design. Try to do this without cutting through the stabilizer on the back, but if you clip it, you can always slide another piece of stabilizer underneath. Put another piece of stabilizer on top and place all layers in the hoop. Using your pattern again behind the hoop, draw the bars on the stabilizer. Proceed with these branched bars as you did with the large cutout.

When you have finished all the bars, change the machine settings. Raise the feed dogs and set the machine on stitch width 2. Use the open embroidery presser foot. Begin sewing at the point of the heart. Anchor the threads and proceed clockwise. As you travel around the curves, stitch very slowly, your machine set on moderate speed. To fill in the curves smoothly, stop with the needle down on the right side, lift the presser-foot lever, pivot the hoop, lower the presser foot, and stitch again. Repeat several times when negotiating curves.

Satin stitch around each cutout. Carefully pull away the stabilizer and rinse out any remaining pieces. Press the embroidery from the back.

Eyelets

I've used eyelets in my embroideries, clumping them together for a center of interest, and one of my teachers uses them to decorate lovely bed linens. Many sewing machine companies offer eyelet plates (see Chapter 1 for more about eyelet makers).

Lesson 13. Free-machined needlelace

The terms *cutwork, lacy spiderwebs,* and *openwork* all describe a machine stitchery technique far removed from darning holes in socks or shredded elbows. But, like darning, they do entail stitching across open spaces.

Openwork is done in a hoop with the fabric stretched tightly. Place the hoop, fabric side down, on the machine bed. Draw a circle on the fabric: Circles are easier to control than the squares, crescents and paisley shapes you may want to try later.

Start stitching at the edge of the circle by bringing the bobbin thread to the top. Anchor the threads by sewing a few stitches in one spot. Guide the hoop slowly as you stitch around the circle three times (Fig. 5.3A). Take the hoop off the machine and, without removing the fabric from it, cut out the circle close to the stitches. If you have opted to use water-soluble stabilizer, now is the time to slip it into the hoop under your fabric. Replace the hoop and secure the threads once again at the edge of the hole.

Now you will begin to lay in a network of spokelike threads across the space. To do this, begin by stitching across from one side of the hole to the other side. Move the hoop slowly, but run the machine moderately fast to strengthen and put a tighter twist on the spoke. When your needle enters the fabric again, move along the circle

---

Stitch width: 0
Stitch length: 0
Needle position: center
Needle: #80
Feed dogs: lowered or covered
Presser foot: darning or no presser foot
Tension: *top,* normal; *bobbin,* normal
Fabric suggestions: any weight
Thread: one color, machine embroidery or polyester
Accessories: 6" (15.2cm) wrapped wooden hoop; water-soluble stabilizer (optional)

to another spot, secure threads, and sew directly across the hole again. Continue in this manner until you have as many spokes as you wish. On the last pass, go up to the center and backstitch right at the center of the wheel to strengthen the web. Starting at that backstitch, fill in the spokes by sewing in ever-widening circles around the center until the "button" is the size you wish it to be (Fig. 5.3C). Sew a few stitches into the button to lock the thread in place and again move to the outside to anchor the threads and complete that spoke.

Would you like a lacier filling? Sew one backstitch over each spoke after crossing it as you stitch around the center. This keeps the threads from slipping to the center. Travel around and around in wider circles till you reach the edge of the hole.

Although there are as many ways to finish off the edges of the spaces as there are ways to fill them with stitches, one of the softest looks is accomplished by straight stitching from the edge of the hole, out past it and back again, moving the hoop back and forth as if stitching sun rays (Fig. 5.3C). You can also use the widest zigzag and accomplish the same rays. Or, satin stitch around the edge and combine that with other embroidery. These are only a few ideas; try some of your own.

If you have used stabilizer, place your embroidery under a faucet and wash it out when your work is completed.

Create your own samples by placing a piece of medium-weight cotton in a hoop and drawing several circles on it. Stitch around one circle three times. Cut out the center. Stitch a spider web in the hole and finish it off on the edges. Go to the next circle and stitch both the center and the edges in a different way from your first sample. Then do another and another until you have many needlelace samples for your notebook. If you're pleased with the result and want to show it off, back with another fabric and use as a tote bag square.

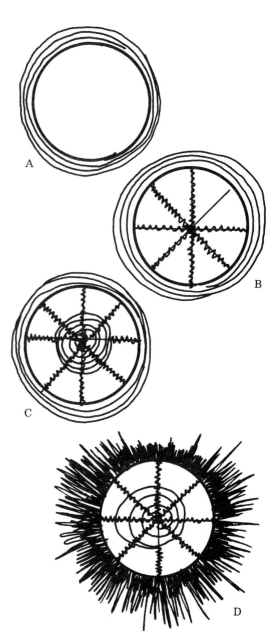

Fig. 5.3 Making needlelace. A. First sew around a circle three times. B. Cut out the center, embroider across the hole, creating spokes. C. Add circles of stitches around the center. D. Stitch radiating lines over the edge, into the fabric.

Lesson 14. Battenberg lace

Battenberg lace was popular in the late 1800s. Straight, machine-made tape was shaped into a design and basted to stiff paper. Then the open spaces were filled with bars and embroidery stitches, which held the tape in shape. After the stitchery was completed, the paper was removed and the Battenberg lace could be used to decorate dresses, curtains or linens.

Project
Paisley-shaped Lace

This lesson will teach you how to make one paisley-shaped piece of Battenberg (Fig. 5.4). From there, you can go on to bigger projects, but let's see if you like Battenberg lacemaking by machine.

There is a variety of white, off-white, black, gold, and silver Battenberg tape to

choose from. It's available by mail-order (see Sources of Supplies) and from some needlework shops.

Should you create your own design, choose a tape that doesn't overpower the

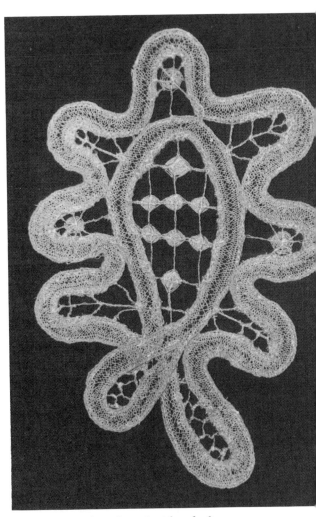

Fig. 5.4 Battenberg is embroidered after narrow tape has been shaped into a design.

Stitch width: 0–1 1/2
Stitch length: 0
Needle position: center
Needle: #90
Feed dogs: lowered
Presser foot: darning foot
Tension: *top,* normal; *bobbin,* normal
Thread: wash-away basting thread;
    #50 (ecru) machine embroidery
Accessories: 7″ (17.8cm) spring hoop;
    water-erasable pen and white permanent marker; ecru Battenberg tape; glue stick; dressmaker's pins
Stabilizer: water-soluble, doubled, large enough for hoop

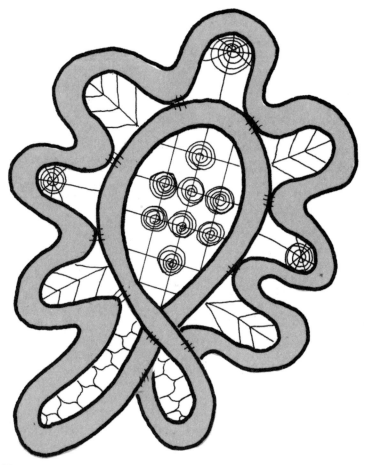

Fig. 5.5 Battenberg pattern.

pattern. The one I used is ¼″ (6.3mm) wide. On each side of the tape is a thread that is thicker than the others. Pull gently to curve the tape into the shape you want.

Place two pieces of water-soluble stabilizer in a hoop and over the design in Fig. 5.5. Trace the outline with a white permanent marking pen. Pull up the thread on the tape, pinning in the shape on the stabilizer as you go. Using glue stick helps to keep edges from curling and holds tape ends in place temporarily. Hide the ends as shown. I find it more satisfactory to baste the design to the stabilizer by hand than by

machine. I use wash-away basting thread for hand basting.

Draw in the stitching lines: Extend them by drawing dots onto the tape with a water-erasable pen. At times the stabilizer may be cut out and these dots can be used for reference.

Set up your machine for free embroidery.

Start by straight stitching around the edge of the tape with machine embroidery thread. When you come to a place that joins a curve to the middle tape, stitch across to the other side and back again. Af-

82

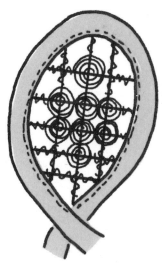

Fig. 5.6 In the center design, first a grid is stitched, then circles are stitched around the crossed threads, as indicated.

the center top. Stitch back over this thread with the machine set on stitch width 1 1/2. Move the hoop quite fast. Don't build up thick bars as in cutwork.

Following the side of the tape (Fig. 5.6), straight stitch to the next mark and stitch to the other side. Follow the tape to the third mark to stitch in the next line. Then stitch around to the side and lay in the other rows of stitches that will cross the first ones. When those are done, zigzag at 1 1/2 stitch width to each cross and stitch a small circle, starting at the center of the crossed thread. Go from one to the next until the center is filled in.

To do the leaves (Fig. 5.7), first cut out the stabilizer if your machine will stitch across open space. Stitch from the center bottom up to the top. Following the side of the tape with straight stitches, stitch to the first branch and then to the center. Take a stitch backward to anchor, then stitch to the other side. Go down to the next branch. Stitch down to the center, anchor, and go up to the other side. Continue in this manner until you finish the last one. Begin to zigzag over the branches, traveling up and back and to the next until they are all covered.

To make the spiderwebs (Fig. 5.8), cut out the stabilizer (or, again, leave it in place), then lay in your threads and zigzag

ter the design is attached, cut out the stabilizer in the center. Be sure your machine can stitch without fabric under the needle. If it can't, then do not cut out the stabilizer. With your machine set up for free embroidery, stitch one long pass from the point at the bottom of the center area up to

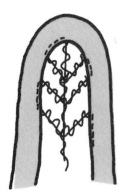

Fig. 5.7 Leaf shapes are filled in with veins called Sorrento bars.

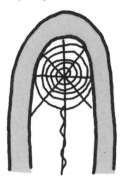

Fig. 5.8 Circles are stitched very closely together at the top of each loop.

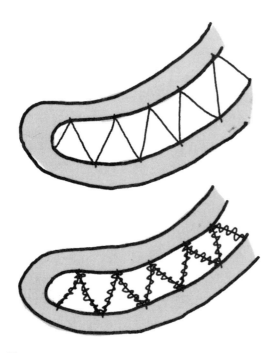

over the center thread. The others will be covered by the circles of stitches that go in next.

Cut out the stabilizer or leave it in the last area (Fig. 5.9). Straight stitch from one side of the tape to the other across the area, then zigzag back with stitch width 1 1/2. At the point where the stitches join the fabric and leave it again, zigzag several stitches over both threads to hold them together. Then travel on over the next thread. Stitch down to the tape, then back over both threads with a few stitches before zigzagging over the next thread to the other side of the tape. Complete this area.

After the lace is stitched, wash out the stabilizer and place the Battenberg between layers of toweling to press.

Fig. 5.9 This fill-in stitch is referred to as Point d'Alençon *when done by hand.*

Lesson 15. Hemstitching

Hemstitching is used on garments and table linens whenever a delicate, feminine look is desired. The technique looks complicated and difficult, but it is surprisingly easy to accomplish using both double- and single-winged needles.

Before you begin to stitch the bonnet, practice on two layers of cotton organdy.

Set up your machine.

To thread two needles, follow instructions in the basic manual for your machine. Remember to always thread your machine with the presser foot up.

Try hemstitching as described in your manual. Start with the single-winged needle and use a zigzag. Stitch a row of hemstitching. At the end of the first run, leave the needle in the hole at left, turn and return, poking into the same holes as on the first run.

You can make an all-over design, covering a large area with hemstitches. This is

Stitch width: 0 to no wider than the throat plate opening when using a double needle
Stitch length: varies
Needle position: center
Needle: single and double hemstitching needles; double needles to match sizes of pintuck feet
Feed dogs: up
Presser foot: open embroidery foot, pintuck feet
Tension: *top,* normal; *bobbin,* normal
Fabric: crisp fabric, such as organdy or linen
Thread: cotton machine embroidery

usually worked on the bias, then appliquéd to something else.

Now practice with the double hemstitch needle. Set up your machine in this way:

Stitch width: 1 3/4
Stitch length: 1 3/4
Needle position: center
Feed dogs: up
Presser foot: open embroidery foot

Make one pass, ending to the left. Lift the presser foot, turn the fabric and stitch the second pass.

Try this blind hemstitch.

Stitch width: 1 3/4
Stitch length: 1 3/4
Needle position: center
Feed dogs: up
Presser foot: open embroidery foot
Built-in stitch: blind hem stitch

Turn your hemstitching into shadow work as well. Cut back the piece of organdy underneath, clipping out both sides of the double fabric on either side of the blind hemstitches.

Project
Infant's Bonnet

I've combined hemstitching with built-in stitches and double needles to make the infant's bonnet shown in Fig. 5.10. Also included is a line of ribbon sewing. This can

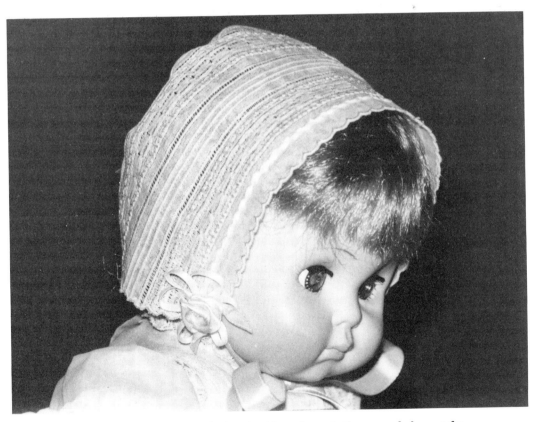

Fig. 5.10 Hemstitching, pintucking, and embroidery decorate the organdy bonnet for an infant or a doll.

Stitch width: varies
Stitch length: varies
Needle position: center, right
Needle: 1.6mm twin needle; single and double hemstitching needles
Feed dogs: up
Presser foot: open embroidery foot; 5-groove pintuck foot
Tension: *top,* normal; *bobbin,* normal
Fabric suggestion: white cotton organdy
Thread: light-blue, fine machine-embroidery thread; #5 light-blue pearl cotton; white cordonnet
Other supplies: pearl bead (optional); ⅛" (3.2mm) double-faced satin ribbon, approximately 1 yard (91.4cm); ¼" (6.3mm) double-faced satin ribbon, ½ yard (45.7cm); ½" (12.7mm) double-faced satin ribbon, approximately 1½ yards (137.2cm)

be made in the time it would take you to shop for a baby gift.

Nora Lou Kampe of LaGrange, Illinois, made this bonnet using embroidered eyelet fabric with a scalloped border–a way to make a baby gift in no more than an hour's time. I used her bonnet idea, but took the long-cut and embroidered the bonnet myself; it fits a newborn and you could make one for a christening. A gown can be done in the same hemstitching technique.

The finished bonnet is 13" × 5¾" (33.0cm × 14.6cm). Add to both width and length if you're adapting it for an older baby.

Begin with two pieces of organdy, each 18" × 9" (45.7cm × 22.9cm). I start with a much larger area than I need because I practice on the margin–running the decorative stitches so they will match when I do a mirror image. If your machine does a mirror image with a push of a button, add the fabric anyway to cut off later for your notebook.

Wash and iron the organdy. Mark the top fabric lengthwise, using a water-erasable marker (Fig. 5.11). Start by marking lines 1" (2.5cm) apart from the front edge. Use a T-square for accuracy. Draw six lines. Then mark a line ½" (12.7mm) from the last line, and another ½" (12.7mm) from that one; 7" × 13" (17.8cm × 33.0cm) is marked. Pin the two pieces of fabric together at the top of the lines.

Once you have learned how to hemstitch, the decoration is up to you. The following is only a suggestion: Thread the double-wing needle with light-blue thread. The first line of blind hemstitches are stitched 1" (2.5cm) from the front edge. Use the blue line as your guide and stitch on top of it. When you reach the end, turn and go back, cutting into the same hole you stitched on the first run. Sew slowly. If the needle does not hit exactly in the right place, stop and move the fabric by one or two threads. Continue.

Spread the fabric apart. The pintucking is done between the blue lines on the top piece only.

Change to the 1.6mm double needle. Use the 5-groove pintuck foot, light-blue #5 pearl cotton, feed dogs up, stitch length 2. Thread the hole in the throat plate with pearl cotton.

There are three lines of pintucking, so stitch the first line exactly in the middle, between the blue marker lines. Stitch the others on either side of this one, using the grooves in the pintuck foot as guides.

If you wish, stitch all four groups of pintucks between the blue lines at one time, then go back, take the pearl cotton out of the throat plate, change to the hemstitching needle, and continue to hemstitch on the blue lines with the blind hemstitch. Remember, when you pintuck, work on one layer of fabric, but hemstitch on both layers.

Complete 4½" (11.4cm) of the bonnet (shaded area on Fig. 5.11) by filling in the empty spaces between the hemstitched blind hem pattern and the pintucks. Use the open effect of the single-wing needle, sewing in a straight line. Remember to come back again, punching holes in the same places where the first ones were.

Should you still want more decoration, use a built-in stitch of your choice. Sew down the sides of the lines of blind hemstitches. When you have decorated the fabric enough, straight stitch around the edge of the bonnet rectangle. Cut back to the stitching line. Put the piece you've practiced on into your notebook.

Fold the bonnet rectangle in half (Fig. 5.12). The fold will be the top of the bonnet. Pin the fabric together, matching decorative stitches so it is exact. Round off the front corners where the rosettes will be sewn (see Fig. 5.12). Open up and stitch 1/8″ (3.2mm) in from the edges of the bottom and front.

Change to a scallop design or satin stitch to stitch the front edge and the sides of the bonnet. Use a cording foot, or one that will guide the cord, size #80 needle, stitch width 4, stitch length 1/2 (or whatever works best for you to cover cord smoothly). Do a sample first.

Thread cordonnet through the hole in the foot. Place the foot with the thread hole on the line of stitching. Hold the cord up slightly as you cover it with stitches.

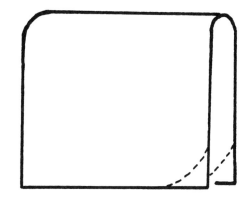

Fig. 5.12 When stitching is completed, fold the rectangle in half and round off the front corners, as shown.

When the scallops are completed, clip fabric back from the edge to the stitching, but not too close to the scallops.

Stitch down on the line 1/2″ (12.7mm) from the edge (back of bonnet) and stitch another 1/2″ (12.7mm) from that line. Fold the back under 1/2″ (12.7mm), then again another 1/2″ (12.7mm). Stitch across the first fold to make the ribbon casing.

Next, wind the bobbin with 1/8″ (3.2mm) double-faced satin ribbon. Tape the end onto the bobbin and begin winding by hand. Finish by winding slowly on the machine. Don't thread it through the spring when full. Instead, bypass the tension

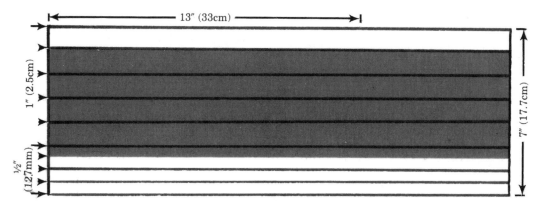

Fig. 5.11 The shaded area of the diagram indicates the portions to be embroidered.

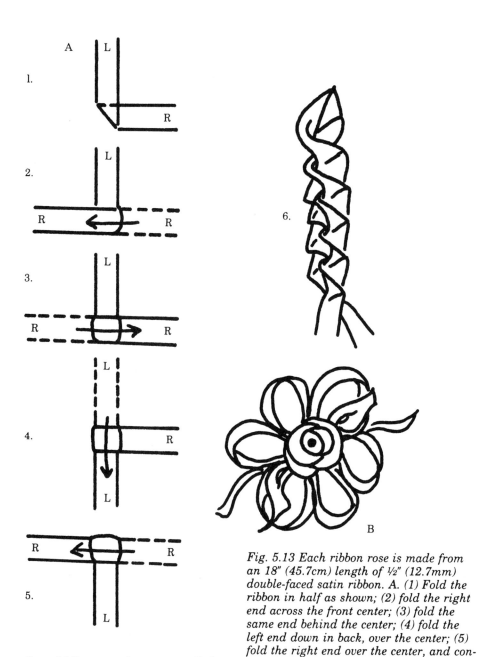

Fig. 5.13 Each ribbon rose is made from an 18" (45.7cm) length of ½" (12.7mm) double-faced satin ribbon. A. (1) Fold the ribbon in half as shown; (2) fold the right end across the front center; (3) fold the same end behind the center; (4) fold the left end down in back, over the center; (5) fold the right end over the center, and continue folding over the center until there are 30 folds between your fingers; (6) holding the last fold between your thumb and forefinger, release the rest of the ribbon, then pull on the ribbon end under the last fold to create the rose. B. By hand, stitch from the back to the center and back again to keep the rose from unwinding. Leave ½" (12.7mm) ends and cut each on a slant. Hold the loops in place with a small ribbon rose or tie small bows at the centers.

spring. (If your bobbin must be wound inside the machine, you will not be able to do this step.) Insert the bobbin into the machine and bring the ribbon to the top. Pull out at least 8″ (20.3cm) of ribbon before beginning to sew. Set the machine for topstitching. Use the 4 stitch length on machines that do not have a topstitch setting.

Use the zigzag foot, tension turned up to 10, and needle position to the right. Place the bonnet front on the bed of the machine. The ribbon will be stitched from underneath, ½″ (12.7mm) from the front edge. When you finish stitching, pull out 8″ (20.3cm) of ribbon and cut off.

If you can't wind ribbon on your bobbin, then attach the ribbon by hand as follows: Leave 8′ of ribbon for a bow and begin tying overhand knots every inch until you have enough knotted ribbon to stretch from one rounded corner to the next across the top front of the bonnet. Then, attach each knot by invisibly stitching it to the bonnet by hand.

Cut two ½″ (12.7mm) satin ribbons, each 12″ (30.5cm) long, for the bonnet ties and attach by stitching several zigzag stitches in one place at the rounded corners under the ⅛″ (3.2mm) ribbon.

Make six loops from the 8″ (20.3cm) of ⅛″ (3.2mm) ribbon. Tack them by hand at the center on top of the ribbon ties. Make ribbon roses as shown in Fig. 5.13A, or tiny bows from the ½″ (12.7mm) ribbon and attach these over the loops by hand (Fig. 5.13B). Use double thread. Poke the

Fig. 5.14 Pull on each end of the back ribbon and tie into a bow to shape the crown of the bonnet.

needle up from the inside of the bonnet, through the ribbon ties, loops, and the center of the flower and a pearl bead. Then poke the needle back through the flower, loops, ribbon tie and bonnet. Do this several times. It's not necessary to go through the bead each time. Anchor the thread underneath.

Thread 18″ (45.7cm) of ¼″ (6.3mm) ribbon through the back casing on the bonnet and pull up to tie into a bow at the back (Fig. 5.14). Cut off at the length you prefer. There you have it—a priceless gift.

Lesson 16. Stitching in rings

Stitching in rings is like making needlelace (Fig. 5.15). Instead of fabric surrounding a space, in this lesson the thread is attached to narrow gold rings. I selected rings about 2½″ (6.4cm) in diameter as an appropriate size for tree ornaments. See Sources of Supplies for ordering these rings.

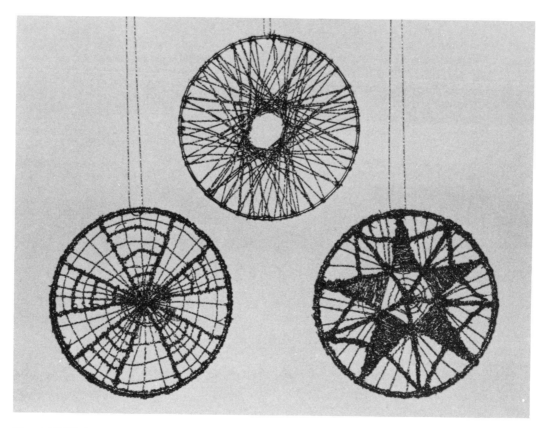

Fig. 5.15 Christmas ornaments stitched in gold rings.

Project Christmas Ornaments

A stabilizer isn't always needed when you sew in space, but it will depend upon your machine. I used to make these Christmas ornaments without a stabilizer and it worked beautifully. But with water-soluble stabilizer underneath, you can stitch more intricate designs, and the thread will stay in one place, as if you were stitching on fabric.

Set up your machine.

Stitch width: 0—4
Stitch length: 0
Needle position: center
Needle: #80
Feed dogs: lowered
Presser foot: bare needle
Tension: *top,* slightly loosened; *bobbin,* normal
Thread: gold metallic on top and bobbin
Accessories: 2½" (6.4cm) gold ring; 7" (17.8cm) spring hoop; permanent white marker
Stabilizer: water-soluble

Double the stabilizer and put it into the hoop. Place the gold ring in the center. Draw a design in the ring.

Dip the needle down at the side of the ring and bring the bobbin thread to the top. Hold the threads to one side. Anchor the ring by hand-walking the needle from the outside to the inside of it. Stitch from one side to the other several times. Hold onto the ring and stitch across to the other side. The chain of stitches will be tighter if you sew fast but move the hoop slowly. Anchor the thread on the other side by sewing over and back on the ring as you did at first.

Work back across and anchor on the other side. Keep doing this until you have laid in the spokes of the design. Remember, with water-soluble stabilizer you can change direction when stitching in open spaces. After the last anchoring stitches, go back into the ring and finish the piece. It can be symmetrical or not. I feel that the lighter the look, the better. Stitching it too thickly will be a detraction, but you may want to zigzag over threads, as in cutwork, to add variety to the design.

Anchor the last stitches and take the ring out of the hoop. Cut back the stabilizer, then dissolve it by holding the ring under running water. Hang it from your Christmas tree with a cord.

Lesson 17. Making Alençon lace

Alençon lace took its name from the French town. The lace was developed there and was so expensive it was rarely seen, except in shops with a wealthy clientele, where it was sold as yardage and used as trimming for lingerie, dresses, and household items.

On the fine, mesh net background is a heavy design, so closely woven it is almost clothlike. Characteristic of Alençon lace is the heavy thread that outlines the design.

Project
Alençon Pincushion

Our Alençon is made on a single layer of bridal veiling. The design is freely embroidered by machine, then outlined with pearl cotton or cordonnet (Fig. 5.16).

Prepare a sample of your stitching to be sure it looks like you want it to. I like a slight bubbly look to the pearl cotton, but you may want a tighter or even looser stitch. If so, tighten or loosen the top tension.

Stitch width: 0
Stitch length: 0
Needle position: center
Needle: #80
Feed dogs: lowered or covered
Presser feet: darning foot and open embroidery foot
Tension: *top*, slightly loosened; *bobbin*, normal
Fabric suggestion: bridal veil, 36" × 5" (91.4cm × 12.7cm); pink satin, 4½" × 11" (11.4cm × 28.0cm)
Thread: #100 or #120 fine white sewing thread; #8 pearl cotton or cordonnet on bobbin to match
Accessories: 7" (17.8cm) spring hoop; permanent white marker; 2 cups of sawdust
Stabilizer: tear-away and water-soluble

Put the water-soluble stabilizer in the hoop. Place it over the design and copy it with the permanent marker (Fig. 5.17). Then place the veiling over the stabilizer in the hoop.

Fig. 5.16 Alençon lace pincushion.

Thread with fine thread in the top and bobbin. Bring the bobbin thread to the top and hold both threads to one side. After stitching a few stitches, clip these ends off. I don't anchor the threads as they will be sewn in anyway. Outline the design first with straight stitches.

When completed, go back and stitch in the petals and leaves. Sew a line next to the outline, then another within that and another, and so on until you have filled it in. If some of the lines overlap, don't despair, as this will happen. Just try to keep from building up heavy stitching lines.

It's not necessary to cut the thread as you complete one section and start another. Loosen the top thread by lifting up on the presser foot and turning the handwheel if necessary. Slowly pull or push the hoop to the next place. There's no need to

bring up the bobbin thread again, as long as it is still connected to the fabric.

When finished stitching, go back and clip threads between motifs. Bring long threads to the back to be clipped and dotted with a drop of Fray-Check. Use tweezers to pull out loose threads on the back.

Change the bobbin to the one containing pearl cotton. Take the veiling out of the hoop and turn it over. The topside of the lace will be underneath. Double check the tensions by sewing on another piece of veiling in another hoop. The pearl cotton should lay flat underneath without pulling; yet it should not be so loose it looks loopy.

Dip the needle into the veil and bring the pearl to the top. Hold it to one side as you begin: Don't anchor it. Outline the design. It is very important to keep from going over lines too many times. You want it to be thick, but not ugly.

When you complete outlining, cut off the pearl cotton, bringing any long ends to the back. Work those under a few stitches on back by hand and clip them off. Put your lace, still in the hoop, under the faucet to wash out the stabilizer.

Measure the top of the pincushion. The finished size will be 4″ × 5″ (10.2cm × 12.7cm) so add ½″ (12.7mm) to each measurement; 4½″ × 5½″ (12.7cm × 14.0cm). Cut two pieces of pink satin this size. Stitch the lace to one of the rectangles. Seam allowance is ¼″ (6.3mm).

Cut a piece of veiling 36″ (91.4cm) long (twice the perimeter of the pincushion), and 5″ (12.7cm) wide. Cut a piece of tearaway stabilizer the same length and 2″ (5.1cm) wide. Pin the cut edges of the veiling together to hold it in place. Slip tearaway under the fold. Set your machine to satin stitch or the scallop stitch (refer to your manual).

Turn feed dogs up. With the right edge of the embroidery foot placed just within the edge of the fold, stitch width 4, length at 1/2 (or whatever would give you an at-

Fig. 5.17 Lace pincushion design.

tractive stitch), sew down the length of the veiling and cut back to the stitching. Wash out the stabilizer.

To gather the ruffle, zigzag over cordonnet (see Lesson 4). Stitch the length of the cut edges (stitch length 2, stitch width 1). Use the cord to gather the ruffle.

Join the two ends of the ruffle by placing one end over the other about ½" (12.7mm). Using a 2 stitch width, and 1/2 length, satin stitch down the width of the piece of veiling. Cut back to the line of stitching on both sides.

Gather the ruffle, placing the seam at a corner. Corners should be heavily gathered to make sure they lay beautifully when completed. Distribute the ruffles around the edge of the pincushion. Re-member that the embroidered edge will be toward the *center* of the pincushion. Stitch in place. It's not necessary to remove the cordonnet.

The last step is to sew the back of the pincushion to the lace. Place right sides together, and work all the net ruffles inside as you pin around the edge.

Sew within the stitching line on front. Leave a large enough opening so you can turn the pincushion to the outside. When turned, fill it very tightly with sawdust (or use another filler, if you prefer). Stitch the opening shut by hand.

Do you like making lace? Try other variations by using built-in stitches, satin-stitch star flowers, or bands of intertwined cordonnet at the edges.

CHAPTER **6**

Drawing Threads Out of Your Fabric

■ **Lesson 18. Needleweaving**

To create an area of free, lacy openwork called needleweaving, first draw threads out of a fabric, then stitch over the remaining threads. On this long-cut, I used exactly the same color thread on the top and bobbin as that of the dress; I'm constantly being asked how it was stitched. The solution to the mystery follows.

Lesson 18. Needleweaving

Because needleweaving is worked in a straight line, I chose to decorate the sleeves of a summer dress (Fig. 6.1). I knew this dress would be washed many times, so I chose a polyester sewing thread for durability. I matched it perfectly, both spool and bobbin, with the fabric.

First do a small sample of needleweaving for your notebook. The openwork is 1″ (2.5cm) wide. Pull out a horizontal thread at the top and the bottom where the openwork will be. Straight stitch across those lines. Then pull out the horizontal or weft threads in that space.

Project
Openwork
on Sleeves

You will machine stitch over the vertical or warp threads, drawing them together as you zigzag (Fig. 6.2).

Take off the regular presser foot and use a bare needle or darning foot. Try working without a hoop on this project. The stitching goes fast and a hoop would only slow you down. You may stitch with water-soluble stabilizer behind your work, but that is optional and depends upon whether your machine will stitch across open space or not. Prepare your machine for embroidery

Stitch width: 0–4
Stitch length: 0–1/2
Needle position: center
Needle: #80
Feed dogs: lowered, up
Presser foot: open embroidery, darning, or no presser foot
Tension: *top*, normal, loosened; *bobbin*, normal
Fabric suggestion: loosely woven
Thread: Metrosene polyester
Stabilizer: tear-away, or construction paper to match thread; water-soluble (optional)

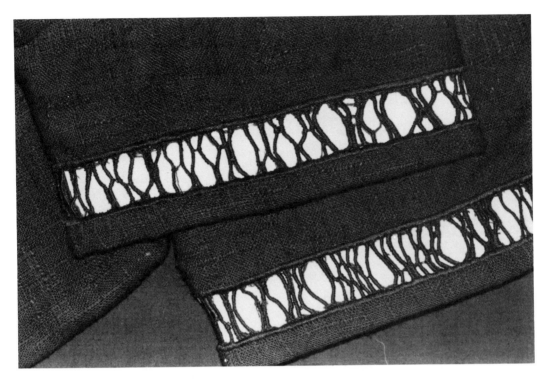

Fig. 6.1 Needleweaving decorates the sleeves on a summer dress.

Fig. 6.2 Pull out warp threads from the fabric and zigzag freely over the remaining wefts. Then finish the edges on each side with satin stitching.

by lowering or covering the feed dogs. Be sure the presser bar is down before you start to stitch. Dip the needle down and bring the bobbin thread to the top. Anchor the threads. Set the machine on stitch width 4 and normal tension.

Using both hands, grasp the top and bottom of the fabric between your fingers, stretching it slightly as you stitch. Keep the fabric as close as you can to the needleplate, and keep tension on the warp threads.

Begin to move from just below the stitched line at the bottom to just over the stitched line on top. Move the fabric slowly, but sew at a comfortable speed, catching several warp threads together as you zigzag to the top.

When you reach the top, move sideways to the next several warp threads and begin stitching those together. About halfway down, move the fabric to the side and catch a few stitches into the previous group of zigzagged threads. Then move back and continue to the bottom of the threads. Finish all the warp threads in the same manner, satin stitching up and down, while at the same time catching threads from the previous run in one or two places. This adds interest and strength to your openwork and is an integral part of your needleweaving.

After finishing, remove water-soluble stabilizer and pull the piece back into shape while damp. Press.

If you did not use stabilizer, then spray with water to enable you to pull it into shape. Press.

Draw two horizontal lines (one inch apart and as long as your needleweaving) across a piece of construction paper or tear-away stabilizer. Place your needleweaving on top of this, using the drawn lines as guides to keep the open area straight.

Set up your machine for straight stitching with feed dogs up and the open embroidery foot on. Sew a line of straight stitches across the top and bottom on the same guidelines you stitched at the beginning. This will hold the needleweaving in place and stabilize it for the final stitching.

Set the machine to a wide zigzag, feed dogs still up, stitch length 1/2 (or whatever will result in a perfect satin stitch). Loosen tension slightly and satin stitch over those lines, covering the edges in two passes — the first narrower and more open than the second. This takes longer, but the results are more professional-looking. The stitching will fall just to one side of the fabric and will catch the fabric on the other side to neatly finish the edge of the needlelace. Tear off the stabilizer and steam press the embroidery carefully.

If the stabilizer can still be seen behind the stitches, it may be possible to remove it by dampening it, then using a tweezers to remove it. Or use this trick: if you can find a permanent marker the same color as the thread, dab in the color where necessary.

Try needleweaving across the yoke or pocket of a blouse, or down the middle of sleeves, or combine two rows of this with lacy spiderweb circles scattered between.

If you don't like the see-through look, or if you want to add another color, back the open area with another fabric.

You are more than halfway through *Know Your Sewing Machine.* Do you know your sewing machine?

CHAPTER 7

Layering Fabrics: Quilting

- **Lesson 19. Quilting with feed dogs up**
- **Lesson 20. Quilting with feed dogs lowered**
- **Lesson 21. Trapunto**
- **Lesson 22. Italian cording**

I've always taken time to make handmade gifts for special people. But if I make a crib quilt, for example, I'd like to know that the baby won't be twice as long as the quilt by the time the gift is presented. If I'm sewing clothes, I'm realistic: I want the garment to be in style when the recipient opens the box.

So, although I love hand quilting and hand sewing, they often take too long. Machine quilting, on the other hand, is speedy and sturdy. You can use heavy fabrics like corduroy, as well as thick batts, and you will have no trouble stitching them together. If machine quilting is done properly, it can be as fine as handwork.

In this chapter I've included quilting with the feed dogs lowered and in place, trapunto, and Italian cording.

Remember several things when doing any type of quilting. The first is to pre-shrink all fabrics. I usually use cotton poly-ester blends for my quilts so they stay new-looking for a long time. Sheets are excellent backing materials. They come in a myriad of colors and prints, can be of excellent quality, and they won't have to be pieced. When I make a quilt, I use a sheet that is larger than the top.

I usually quilt with a polyester sewing thread. Most brands come in a wealth of colors. Should I want to emphasize the stitching line, I will double the thread. But when I sew on a patterned material or a fabric that changes color throughout, I choose a monofilament. I may or may not use monofilament on the bobbin, depending upon the samples I do first.

Using safety pins instead of hand basting is my favorite method of holding the fabrics and batt together before I quilt. I don't use dressmaker's pins because many of them fall out before the quilt is completed—and those that don't usually stab me.

Lesson 19. Quilting with feed dogs up

Instead of a regular presser foot, I use an even-feed or walking foot when I sew lines of straight quilting stitches. It minimizes puckering on the backing fabric, as the top and bottom fabrics are fed through at the same speed with no slipping.

Before I had one of those helpful attach-ments, I grasped the quilt in both hands and kept it taut as it fed through the machine. As I progressed, I stopped and looked underneath to be sure I had a smooth lining. I must admit I became an expert at sewing without puckers. It may take a little longer, but the lack of a walking foot should not deter you from starting your first quilt experiment.

Can you imagine how fast you could make a quilt using striped fabric or a striped sheet for the top? Use the stripes as quilting lines. If you use stripes for garments, keep in mind that the more rows of quilting, the smaller the piece becomes. I either quilt the fabric first and then cut out the pattern, or I cut my pattern larger than necessary, do the quilting and then lay the pattern back on it when finished. I recut the pattern where necessary.

If you piece a quilt and decide to machine quilt it by using stitch-in-a-ditch, you may prefer using the edging foot or blind hem foot with a black bar extension. Stitch-in-a-ditch is done on top of the quilt by stitching in the seam lines (the ditches). With these presser feet, it is easy to stitch exactly in the ditch because you have the black bar guides and the needle positioning dial for accuracy.

Project
Tote Bag Square (Appliqué and Quilting)

This quilted sample can be used as a square for the tote bag in Chapter 12. It includes appliqué, satin stitches, and sewing with feed dogs up and lowered (Fig. 7.1).

There are five fabrics used in this quilted square. The patterned fabric in the center contains red, blue, green and yellow—all the colors used in the four corners. Use the center fabric, the patterned one, as backing. Using the Teflon sheet, iron fusible webbing onto each of the plain colored fabrics.

Trace the design in Fig. 7.1 and cut apart. Place each piece on fabric and draw around it with a water-erasable marker.

Have you noticed how butting pieces of appliqué next to each other usually leaves gaping areas, no matter how careful you are? To prevent this, plan to overlap adjacent pieces by ¼" so you don't have two raw edges to sew over. Decide ahead of time which side of each piece will have a seam allowance that can be slipped under the corner fabric next to it. If you use this method, you'll have only one edge to cover with satin stitches.

Back the piece with fleecy Pellon, slightly larger than the square, and under that slip a piece of tear-away stabilizer. Use one of the four colors of machine embroidery thread to attach your appliqués.

Dial down the satin stitch to a hair narrower and shorter than the numbers you will use on the second and final pass. On the second pass, use a stitch width 4 and close satin-stitch length. Sew at a moderate speed and always turn with the needle in the fabric.

When you have finished satin stitching the fabric in place, go back and stitch (stitch width 0, stitch length 2) down each side of the satin stitches. This not only

Stitch width: 0–4
Stitch length: 0–2
Needle position: center
Feed dogs: up and lowered or covered
Presser foot: open embroidery, darning
Needle: #80
Tension: *top*, slightly loosened; *bobbin*, normal
Thread: cotton machine embroidery
Fabric: one 9" (23cm) square of lightweight printed cotton; four 6" (15.2cm) squares in different colors; 10" (25.4cm) square of fleece
Accessories: water-erasable marker; fusible webbing; ruler; Teflon pressing sheet; tracing paper and pencil
Stabilizer: heavy tear-away

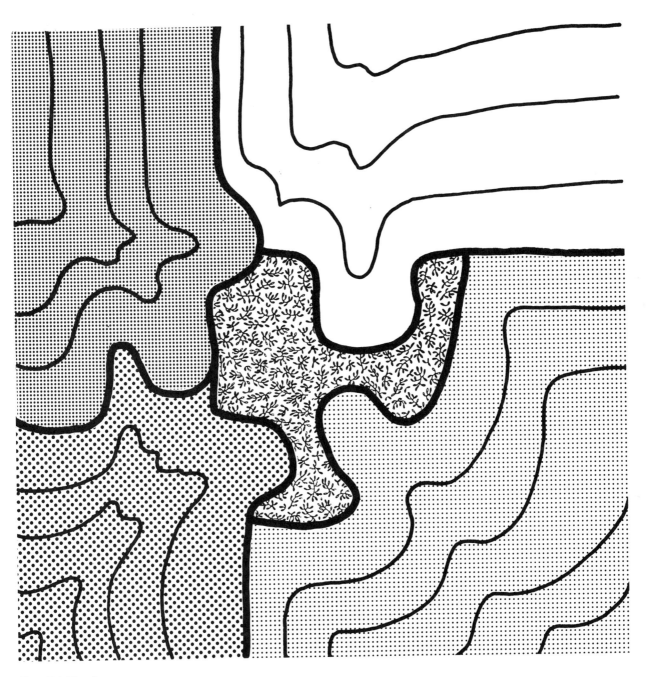

Fig. 7.1 Tote bag square.

adds to the quilted look, but it gives the satin stitches a clean finish.

If you have a machine that balks at bulk, an alternative method is to finish the appliqué first, then place the finished piece over the fleecy Pellon to quilt by straight-stitching the edges of the satin stitches.

Then echo quilt the square, using a color that matches each fabric (or use monofilament thread). Lower or cover the feed dogs and use the darning foot to free-machine quilt lines ½″ apart.

Finish the square as described in Chapter 12.

Lesson 20. Quilting with feed dogs lowered

As you can tell from the lesson title, this will be free-machine quilting. The machine setting will not control the length of the stitches; you will. If you move the fabric fast, the stitches will be longer than if you move it slowly. Not working in a hoop, you must use a darning foot to prevent skipped stitches. And no hoop means you must hold the fabric taut while stitching.

One of the easiest ways to learn free quilting and to practice control at the same time is to quilt around the motifs of a printed fabric as shown in Fig. 7.2. Even the underside looks terrific: you may like the looks of the lining better than the printed side. If so, it makes for a stunning reversible jacket.

When quilting any fabrics with feed dogs lowered, don't place the stitching lines too closely together, unless you want to em-

phasize the area that *isn't* stitched. Closely stitched, it will be too stiff and you'll lose the contrast of light and dark shadowing that makes this type of machining so effective.

Fig. 7.2 *Cotton print, batting and velveteen are quilted together by stitching the butterfly design.*

Stitch width: 0
Stitch length: 0
Needle position: center
Needle: #90
Feed dogs: lowered or covered
Presser foot: darning foot
Tension: *top,* slightly loosened; *bottom,* normal
Fabric suggestion: medium-weight cotton; fleece or quilt batting
Thread: machine embroidery
Accessories: water-erasable marker

Lesson 21. Trapunto

In trapunto, two pieces of fabric are stitched together, following a design. Then the quilter selects the areas of the design to be stuffed with fiberfill. Usually trapunto is done from underneath the fabrics.

Layer two pieces of material together and use the felt flower design in Fig. 4.5 (Lesson 10). Transfer the design to the top fabric. Place both fabrics in a hoop. Stitch in the design, using machine embroidery thread the same color as the fabric, with your machine set up for free-machine embroidery or feed dogs up and embroidery foot on. Stitch in the design. Make small slits in the backing fabric behind the petals, leaves, or stamens—or all three. Add fiberfill, poking it in with a tool that is not sharply pointed. Whip stitch the slits closed by hand.

You can trapunto from the top by appliquéing on top of a base fabric. Slip filling inside the appliqué before you've attached it all the way around. You may want to add stitches over the surface of the appliqué to hold the stuffing firmly and to embellish the design.

Lesson 22. Italian cording

Italian cording is often mistaken for trapunto. The difference is that the area to be stuffed in Italian cording will be the space between two stitching lines. Instead of using fiberfill, thread a cord of appropriate size through the double lines of stitching.

It's also possible to create the look of Italian cording in one pass of the machine, on one layer of fabric when stitching with a double needle. Thread gimp or pearl cotton through the needle plate of your machine and it will be caught between the lines of stitching by the bobbin thread.

Project
Tote Bag Square (Italian Cording)

This square (Fig. 7.3) was done using a single needle.

Draw your design on the fabric with a water-erasable marker, indicating where

Stitch width: 0
Stitch length: 2
Needle position: center
Needle: #80 sharp
Feed dogs: up
Presser foot: open embroidery foot
Tension: *top,* normal; *bobbin,* normal
Fabric suggestions: lightweight cotton for top; stiffer cotton for backing
Thread: shiny rayon or machine embroidery cotton
Cord: appropriate-size acrylic yarn or cable cord
Accessories: hand-sewing needle; large-eyed hand-sewing tapestry needle to thread cord through the design; water-erasable marker

the lines will cross and which ones cross over, which under.

When you are stitching the lines, don't anchor threads when the lines cross. Instead, pull several inches of thread out of the needle. Hold the thread to one side. Skip over the intersection; then begin

Fig. 7.3 Italian cording tote bag square.

stitching again. When finished, go back and clip the threads in the middle. Thread up a sewing needle and poke all the top threads through to the back and work them in. Finish up by working the cord through the design by hand.

It's difficult to turn corners with cording and make those corners look sharp. Poke the needle out of the back fabric at a corner, and then back in again in the same place, leaving a small loop of the cord out in back.

When working with a double needle, turn corners in three steps. Stitch to the corner. Stop. Needles should be grazing the fabric. Lift the presser foot. Half-turn the fabric. Lower the presser foot and turn the wheel by hand to make one stitch. Raise the needles and again bring the needle points down to barely touch the top of the fabric. Lift the presser foot again and complete the turn. Lower the presser foot and continue stitching.

Directions for finishing the square are in Chapter 12.

Look for inspirations for trapunto in books on Celtic designs or bargello borders.

CHAPTER **8**

Adding Interesting Seams
to Your Fabric

- **Lesson 23. French handsewing by machine**
- **Lesson 24. Seaming with feed dogs up and lowered**

In previous chapters, the emphasis was on decorative stitchery. In Chapters 8 and 9, the focus is on sewing. The chapters are so closely related that at times they even overlap. Included in Chapters 8 and 9 are many of the sewing long-cuts I mentioned in the Preface and Chapter 1. But now, instead of decorating a garment by embroidering or appliquéing on it, you'll learn to make the garment unique by changing the seams, hems and edges.

Let's face it: seams are not always interesting. Most of them are hidden and it's not necessary that they do anything but hold two pieces of fabric together. On the other hand, seams can be the focal point of your creation. This chapter includes seams for the finest lace to the heaviest canvas— seams purely practical and those that combine decoration with practicality. Stitch up samples of all of them for your notebook. You'll discover that knowing your sewing machine is a joy.

The project in this chapter is a wedding handkerchief (Fig. 8.1). After learning how to accomplish French handsewing on the machine, work this project. It can also be used as a pillow top.

Lesson 23. French handsewing by machine

When I first heard about the type of clothing construction called French handsewing, I thought it was something new–until Marcia Strickland, a friend from Birmingham, Alabama, showed me her daughters' dresses. They were made of laces, with pintucks and embroidery, entredeaux and hemstitching, and looked like our family's christening gown. I knew French handsewing; I just hadn't been acquainted with the term. We'd always called it "sewing by hand" and I had agonized over it years ago, when I was sure I'd be struck blind by the tiny stitches before I made it through junior high school. It was

hard for me to believe that I could accomplish the perfection of Marcia's clothing on my sewing machine (called "French handsewing by machine" or "French machine sewing").

It's possible to find lace and tucked blouses, skirts and dresses in any department store today. Because this feminine look is expensive in ready-to-wear, if you learn the following hand-sewing techniques by machine and sew them yourself, you will save money and have a lot of fun besides.

First, I had to learn basics before I could stitch collars or dresses. Marcia taught me that if I apply fabric to lace, one of the rules of French handsewing is that I must always have entredeaux between.

Entredeaux literally means "between two." It is purchased by the yard in fabric shops. The fabric on either side of the ladderlike strip down the center is trimmed off before it is attached. I also learned that the holes in entredeaux are never evenly spaced, no matter how expensive it is.

Marcia suggested size 100 pure cotton thread and #70 needle for sewing. She uses an extra-fine thread because the batiste fabric used is extremely lightweight, and stitches are visible when attaching lace and entredeaux or stitching pintucks. And she suggests using cotton thread for heirlooms because it will last a long time.

When handsewing, Marcia chooses cotton batiste because it is easier to roll and whip the edges of cotton. Polyester or cotton/polyester blends have minds of their own. It's hard to roll them as they keep unrolling while you try to whip them in place.

But French machine sewing can easily be done on blends, so I often choose a cotton/polyester for fabric (and thread), as it doesn't wrinkle like pure cotton.

I learned so much from Marcia, I filled a notebook with samples, ideas, and shortcuts. When you stitch up samples for your own notebook, if a technique can be done several ways, do them all and then decide which works best for you. The following techniques are all you need to learn for French machine sewing.

Sewing French seams

French seams are used on lightweight, transparent fabrics to finish the seams beautifully, disguising raw edges. They are also found on smocked garments as a fine finish.

The seams are accomplished in two different operations (Fig. 8.2). Begin with fabric pieces, right sides facing. Stitch the

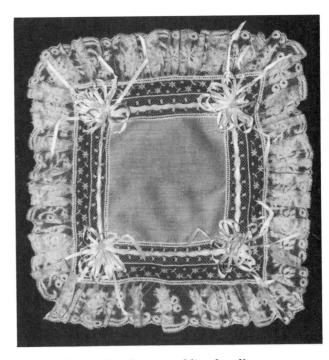

Fig. 8.1 French hand-sewn wedding handkerchief stitched on my Bernina.

seam, using a #70 needle and fine sewing thread. Open and press seam to one side. Cut back the seam allowance evenly, to ⅛" (3.2mm). Turn the fabric back over the raw edges, press again (the seam will be at the edge), pin, and stitch again, enclosing the ⅛" (3.2mm) seam allowance.

The Bernina Cut'n'Sew accessory produces an exceptionally clean French seam. As you sew the seam on the first pass, the fabric is also trimmed to ⅛" (3.2mm), without the uneven edge that sometimes occurs when you cut by hand. When the fabric is folded back over the seam allowance, no maddening wispy threads poke out to ruin the perfect French seam.

Stitching rolled and whipped edges

Rolled and whipped edges (Fig. 8.3) are always used in conjunction with French

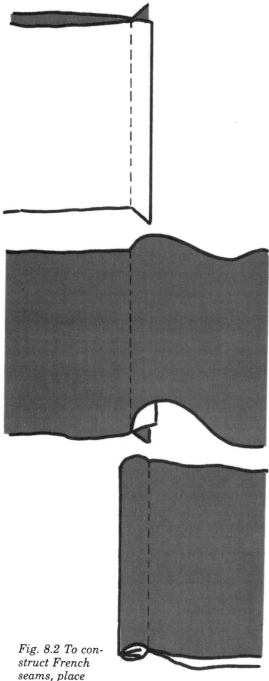

handsewing because each piece of fabric must have a finished edge before it is attached to lace or to entredeaux. When working by machine, sometimes you can finish the edge at the same time you attach it to the lace. These edges can be worked several ways and everyone seems to have her own favorite.

Settings for both the buttonhole foot and the zigzag foot follow:

	Buttonhole Foot	Zigzag Foot
Stitch width	2 1/2	2 1/2
Stitch length	1	1
Needle position	far left	center
Needle	#70	#70
Feed dogs	up	up
Tension		
top	normal	normal
bobbin	normal	normal
Fabric	batiste	batiste
Thread	#100 cotton	#100 cotton

Start the edge so even the first thread in the fabric will be rolled and whipped: Feed a small piece of scrap fabric—about 2″ (5.1cm) long—under the foot. Use the same fabric you will be sewing on. The edge should be placed to the right of the center of both the buttonhole and zigzag foot.

Stitch, holding the threads from the top and bobbin until the fabric begins to roll. As it rolls and as you approach the end of the scrap fabric, butt the good fabric up to it (see Fig. 8.3). It will also roll, beginning exactly at the edge. Later you will cut off the scrap fabric.

I like working a rolled and whipped edge with the foot (pin removed) from the Ber-

Fig. 8.2 To construct French seams, place fabrics wrong sides together, stitch the seam, trim to ⅛″ (3.2mm), then fold the fabric back over the seam allowance and stitch down outside the allowance.

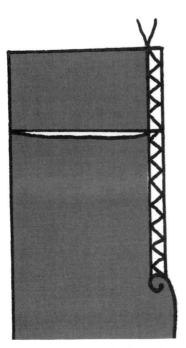

Fig. 8.3 Rolled and whipped edges, started by stitching first on a piece of scrap fabric, then placing the good fabric directly in front of the scrap to begin the roll and whip at the edge.

To start the fabric when using the Cut'n'Sew attachment, first cut a notch in the fabric by clipping from the top down the cutting line ⅜″ (1cm). Tuck this piece to the right of the knife or cut it off. Slip the fabric into the Cut'n'Sew and sew a few stitches. Hold onto the threads to guide the fabric through.

Gathering rolled and whipped edges

Before you roll and whip, stitch (stitch length 2) along the edge of the fabric. Instead of anchoring your threads, leave several inches of thread at the beginning and end of the stitching. Starting at the top again, overcast the edge as you did before rolling and whipping (Fig. 8.4A). The

nina Cut'n'Sew accessory. I've used the same settings with a straight appliqué foot with the same excellent results.

Stitch width: 4
Stitch length: 1
Needle position: right
Tension: *top,* 10; *bobbin,* normal
Fabric: batiste, work on wrong side
Presser foot: remove pin from Cut'n'Sew foot or use straight-toed appliqué foot

Fig. 8.4 Gathering a rolled and whipped edge. A. Sew a line of straight stitches along the edge of the fabric, then roll and whip over the line of stitching. B. Gather the material by pulling on the top thread from the line of straight stitches.

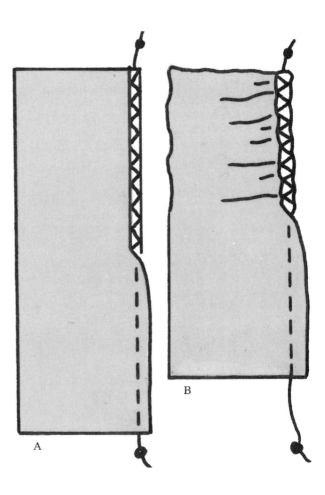

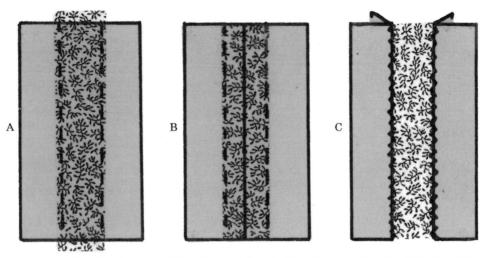

Fig. 8.5 A. Sew lace insert to fabric by straight stitching down each side of the lace. B. Cut through the fabric behind the lace from top to bottom. C. Turn back the seam allowances on both sides and zigzag down the edges of the insertion. Trim the seam allowances back to the stitching.

straight stitching must not be caught in these zigzags.

Hold the thread ends at the beginning of your line of straight stitching to keep them from slipping through as you gather. Pull on the top thread at the other end of the line of straight stitches and evenly distribute the ruffling (Fig. 8.4B).

Applying insertion

Insertion is lace with two straight sides. It is easily applied by machine (Fig. 8.5). Draw two lines the width of the lace on the fabric. Pin the lace inside the lines. Machine straight stitch down both sides of the lace to hold it in place. Cut straight down the fabric behind the lace, allowing seam

Fig. 8.6 Join two pieces of lace together by overlapping the design at each end, zigzagging the "seam," then cutting back the surplus lace to the stitches.

108

allowance on fabric. Fold the seam allowances back and press.

Then zigzag over the edges of the lace and the straight stitching to attach the lace and finish the edges simultaneously. Cut the seam allowances back to the stitching.

Apply scalloped lace as an insertion by placing it on the fabric and basting it down both sides. Cut down the fabric behind. Zigzag closely over the edge, following the scallop. Cut away the fabric underneath. This method can also be used for straight-edge insertion, but the join will not be as strong as folding back the seam allowance and stitching over the doubled fabric.

Joining scalloped lace

Find the most heavily patterned place in the design to join scalloped lace. Overlap two identical patterns, and stitch a fine zigzag (stitch width 1 1/2, stitch length 3/4) with feed dogs up. Follow the edge of the design as shown in Fig. 8.6. Trim back to the line of stitching.

Using entredeaux

Entredeaux is used between fabric and lace. Only the ladderlike strip of stitching down the center of the entredeaux is attached.

Stitch width: 2 or adjust
Stitch length: 1 – 1 1/4
Needle position: center
Needle: #70
Feed dogs: up
Presser foot: buttonhole or zigzag
Tension: *top,* normal; *bobbin,* normal
Fabric suggestions: batiste
Thread: #100

Measure the length of entredeaux you will need and cut off the fabric on only one side. Attach that side. Place the topside of the entredeaux to the topside of the rolled and whipped edge, the entredeaux on top, as shown at left in Fig. 8.7. Be sure the edges touch. Hand walk the machine

through the first couple of stitches to be sure the needle is clearing the edge on the right side and falls into the holes of the entredeaux on the left (Fig. 8.7). Don't worry if the needle skips a hole in the entredeaux once in awhile, because it won't show. If possible, sew with the machine set on moderate speed. When finished, pull the entredeaux to the side away from the fabric and press (at right in Fig. 8.7). Repeat for the other side.

Gathering lace edging

There are several threads at the edges of lace. Use a pin to find the one that gathers the lace and then pull up the thread. Hold onto both ends of this thread, or you might pull it all the way through when gathering the lace. Evenly space the gathers.

Attaching straight-edged lace to rolled and whipped edges

Place the topside of the lace against the topside of the fabric (Fig. 8.8). Be sure the edges are even. Use a zigzag at a setting of stitch width 2 1/2 and length 1. The needle should stitch within the edges of lace and fabric on the left, and stitch off of them on the right swing (Fig. 8.8). Flatten out and press.

Attaching entredeaux to lace insertion

Stitch width: 2, or adjust
Stitch length: 1, or adjust
Presser foot: buttonhole, zigzag, or edging foot with black bar extension down center

Trim fabric from one side of the entredeaux. With topsides up, place the trimmed edge of the entredeaux up next to the edge of the lace.

Zigzag the edges together so the needle barely catches the lace and goes into each hole of the entredeaux (Fig. 8.9). Start by using a 2 stitch width and 1 stitch length,

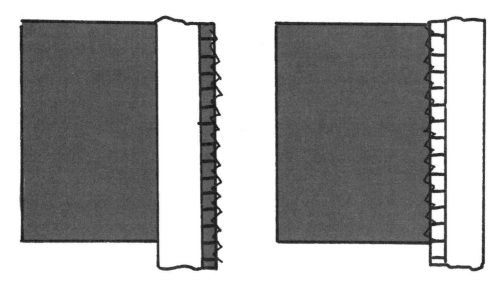

Fig. 8.7 To apply entredeaux to rolled and whipped edges, place it on the fabric, right sides together. Zigzag into each hole and off the edges. Then press open.

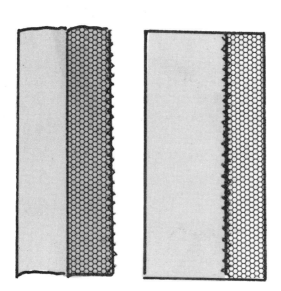

Fig. 8.8 Place insertion on top of a rolled and whipped edge; zigzag to attach. Press open.

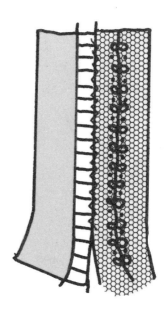

Fig. 8.9 To attach entredeaux to lace insertion, place edges next to each other and zigzag together.

but make adjustments in these figures if you find they are needed.

You can use the edging foot, too. Put entredeaux on one side of the black bar extension, the lace on the other. Set the stitch width to catch both sides as you stitch. The extension on the edging foot helps keep the entredeaux and lace apart until stitched.

Sewing lace to lace

Stitch width: 2 1/2
Stitch length: 1
Presser foot: edging foot with center black bar extension or zigzag foot

Put a strip of straight-edged lace on each side of the edging foot. Stitch between the lace pieces. This foot will keep the lace separated until stitched, so one will not overlap the other.

If you don't have the edging foot, you can use the zigzag foot and butt the edges of the two laces. Use stitch width 3, stitch length 2. Sew the length of the lace.

Fagoting

There are times when we need different detailing on a bodice, sleeve or skirt. It may not be called for in the pattern, but it's a way to make that garment our own, so we choose to take a long-cut and add a creative touch of our choosing to the original pattern.

Fagoting is one way to change a seam or add one. With your machine, you need only a tailor tacking foot, since it's like making fringe.

Stitch width: 2
Stitch length: 1/2
Presser foot: tailor tacking, open embroidery

Make a sample first. Set up your machine by taking your thread out of tension. To do this, follow directions in your manual. If they are not included, try loosening the top tension on your machine.

Place two pieces of fabric together, with right sides facing. Stitch along the seam line. When the line is completed, pull the seam open to reveal the stitches. Change to an embroidery foot and put stabilizer underneath your work. Choose a decorative stitch or even straight stitch to sew each side of the fabric close to the fold.

Go even further with fagoting and bundle the stitches: Sew down the center of the openwork over four stitches with a free-machine straight stitch, back up, and go forward again, stitching past the first bundle and four more stitches (Fig. 8.10). Back up over those four stitches, then stitch forward and over four more stitches. Continue like this until you finish bundling all the stitches.

If your machine has a triple straight stitch, the backward–forward motion will bundle the middle section automatically.

Use fagoting above the hem of a skirt or around a sleeve or square collar.

Fig. 8.10 Fagoting and bundling stitches for an open seam.

111

Project
Wedding
Handkerchief

Many of the techniques you have learned for French machine sewing will be used to make the handkerchief (see Fig. 8.1). You will need: 5″ (12.7cm) square of fine batiste; ½″ (12.7mm) lace insertion; 1″ (2.5cm) beading; entredeaux; lace edging; ⅛″ (3.2mm) double-face satin ribbon, about 6 yards (5.5m); a ruler and water-erasable marker.

How to figure exact amounts of lace and entredeaux is included in the directions be-

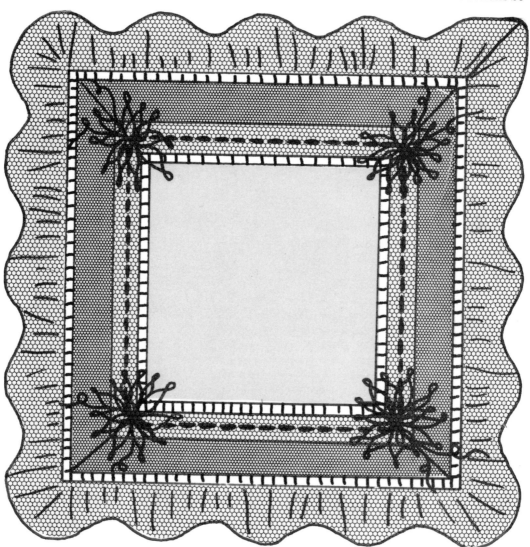

Fig. 8.11 Wedding handkerchief pattern (see also Fig. 8.1)

low; the width of your lace will determine the length you will need. Use a #70 needle and #100 sewing thread.

For the center of this handkerchief (Fig. 8.11), I rolled and whipped a 5″ (12.7cm) square of batiste. Use the method you prefer. Entredeaux was added to the edges; do one side of entredeaux at a time, cut and overlap the openings of the entredeaux at the corners.

Stitch the beading (the lace with holes for threaded ribbon) and lace strip together before attaching them to the entredeaux. Together, the strip of lace is 1½″ (3.8cm) wide.

Estimate how much lace you'll need for your wedding handkerchief by first measuring around the center square of batiste and entredeaux; the example is approximately 20″ (50.8cm).

Double the width measurement of the strip of lace you've made when you

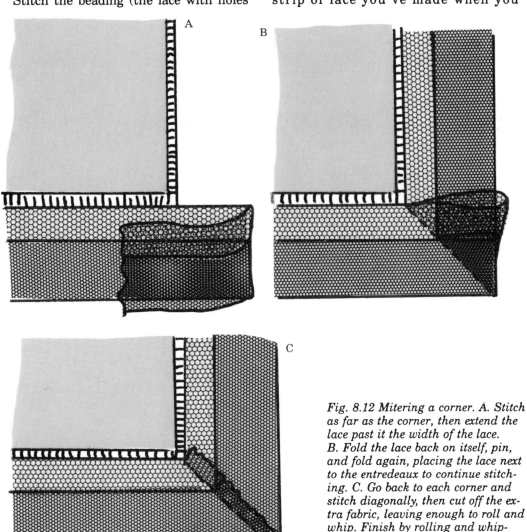

Fig. 8.12 Mitering a corner. A. Stitch as far as the corner, then extend the lace past it the width of the lace. B. Fold the lace back on itself, pin, and fold again, placing the lace next to the entredeaux to continue stitching. C. Go back to each corner and stitch diagonally, then cut off the extra fabric, leaving enough to roll and whip. Finish by rolling and whipping each corner.

stitched the beading to the lace insertion: 1½″ × 2 = 3″ (3.8cm × 2 = 7.6cm).

Multiply 3″ × 4 = 12″ (7.6cm × 4 = 30.5cm) to arrive at the number of inches (cm) needed for the corner miters.

Add the distance around the center square (20″ or 50.8cm) to the corner miters (12″ or 30.5cm). Exact measurement of the lace needed is 32″ (81.3cm). Add 2″ (5.1cm) more for safety.

Leave 2″ (5.1cm) of lace at the corner before you begin attaching lace to the entredeaux (Fig. 8.12). Trim the entredeaux. Place the edge of the lace strip next to the entredeaux so the edges touch (see Fig. 8-12A). Stitch along the first side, ending with needle down at the corner, extending the lace 1½″ (3.8cm) beyond the corner (this is the width measurement of the strip of lace I used). Raise the presser foot. Fold the lace back on itself by the same measurement, 1½″ (3.8cm) or the width of your lace. Pin the lace together at the corner and then fold the lace so it will lie at the edge of the entredeaux on the next side you will stitch (Fig. 8.12B). Turn your work to continue stitching, and put the presser foot down. Hand-walk the first stitch to be sure it catches the lace. Continue stitching slowly to the next corner. Attach lace to the other sides as you did the first.

After the strip of lace has been attached, go back to each corner and fold the lace diagonally to miter it. Check carefully that the corners will lie flat. Pin each one. Mark with a ruler and water-erasable pen where the line of stitching will be (Fig. 8.12B). Sew down the line with a straight stitch before cutting back, leaving enough lace to roll and whip by machine (Fig. 8.12C).

Attach entredeaux to the edge of the lace, overlapping the holes of each piece at the corners, as done previously.

Measure around the outside edge. Double this for the gathered lace measurement. Sew the ends of the lace together by overlapping and at the same time, matching the designs top and bottom. Sew a narrow zigzag along the design and cut back to the line. Place this seam in a corner.

Gather the lace edging by pulling the correct thread and attaching it to the entredeaux. Pin the gathered lace to the entredeaux first to adjust the gathers. Keep the corners of the lace ruffle quite full. Next, stitch the lace to the entredeaux. This can be done in two ways: (1) Place entredeaux on top of the gathered lace, topsides together. Line up the edges and proceed as if attaching the entredeaux

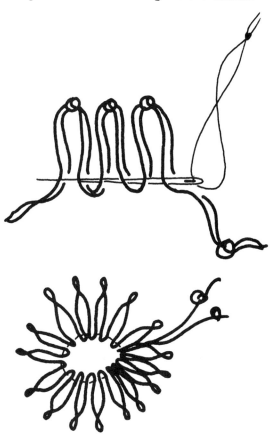

Fig. 8.13 To make a rosette, tie overhand knots in the ribbon every 2½″ (6.4cm). Fold the ribbon into loops with knots at the tops. Sew through each loop, then pull into a rosette.

to rolled and whipped edges; or (2) Place gathered lace next to the entredeaux, topsides up, and zigzag stitch as you did in "Attaching Entredeaux to Lace Insertion."

Thread 1/8" (3.2mm) double-faced satin ribbon through each of the four sides. Leave 3" (7.6cm) tails at each end. Tie overhand knots at the ends. Stitch the tails in place by hand to keep the ribbon in place.

Make rosettes for each corner (Fig. 8.13): First tie an overhand knot every 2½" (6.4cm) along a length of ribbon until you have 16 knots. Leave long ends. Use a double-threaded needle. Make loops on the needle by arranging the ribbon with knots at the top (Fig. 8.13). Sew back through all of the loops again. Pull up and attach the rosettes to the corners of the handkerchief. Tie knots at the ends of the ribbons.

Lesson 24. Seaming with feed dogs up and lowered

Using a lap hemmer

Why is this foot called a hemmer when it is really a seamer? And why is it so infrequently used? It sews seams that are used for strength and decoration. Using the feller (or *felling foot*, other names for it), makes a seam that looks good on both sides (Fig. 8.14).

Use a narrow lap hemmer (4mm seam) for shirt-weight material. If you want a wider seam for denim weights, then buy the lapped hemmer for an 8mm seam.

To use the narrow hemmer, pin two pieces of fabric together so the fabric underneath projects 1/8" (3.2mm) beyond the top piece (Fig. 8.14A). Fold the 1/8" (3.2mm) over the top piece and sew a few stitches (8.14B). Leave the needle in the

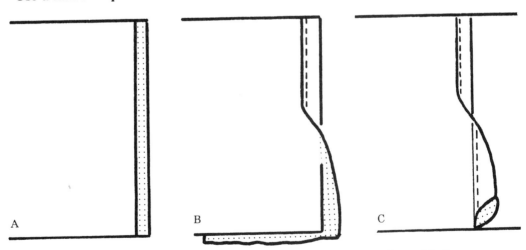

Fig. 8.14 Constructing a lapped hem. A. Place two pieces of fabric together, with the underneath fabric extending beyond the top. B. Use the lap hemmer to stitch the first seam, overlapping the top fabric. C. Open the fabric for the second pass, which will hold the seam in place.

fabric. Lift the hemmer so you can slide the fabric into it. Stitch the seam. Guide the fabric carefully so it feeds evenly.

Iron the seam. Open up the fabric. Again put it into the hemmer. Pull gently away from the seam on both sides as you guide the seam through the presser foot for the second time. The second line of stitching finishes the seam so it will lie flat (Fig. 8.14C).

For a wider seam, let the bottom layer of fabric project ¼" (6.3mm) beyond the top piece.

Sewing a fake lapped hem

If you don't have the felling foot, then sew a ⅝" (15.9mm) seam and press the fabric to the left (Fig. 8.15A, B).

Using the edging foot or blind stitch foot with the black bar extension, place the black bar in the ditch or seam line, needle position to the near left. It will be about ⅛" (3.2mm) from the ditch. Stitch.

For the second run, place the guide on the first stitched line, needle to the far left, and sew a fake-felled seam (Fig. 8.15C).

Of course, you can stitch fake lapped hems with just the zigzag or straight stitch foot. It's possible to use the edge of some presser feet as a measure. Or, mark the stitching lines with a water-erasable marker.

Seaming with a Cut'n'Sew or side-cutter

The Cut'n'Sew or side-cutter is wonderful for cutting fabric and overcasting it in one operation (it's a little like turning your

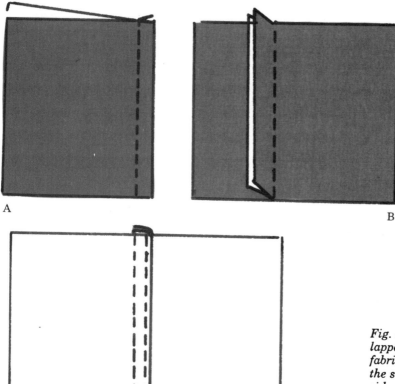

A

B

C

Fig. 8.15 Sewing a fake lapped hem. A. Seam two fabrics together. B. Fold the seam allowance to one side. C. Stitch down the allowance from the right side.

sewing machine into a serger). I didn't think I needed one until it was given to me as a gift. Now I use it constantly. You'll want to use it with many of the practical stitches, such as overlock, double overlock and zigzag. One limitation is the type of fabric it will accept. I could not sew the canvas tote bag with it—it doesn't like tough, tightly woven fabrics.

Stitching over thread on knits

No more stretched-out seams on knits and jerseys when you use this method.

Stitch width: 2
Stitch length: 1
Needle position: center
Needle: #80
Feed dogs: up
Presser foot: cording foot or embroidery pintuck, or zigzag hemmer
Tension: *top*, normal; *bobbin*, normal
Thread: polyester sewing

With a separate spool of thread, thread polyester through the hole or in the groove in the presser foot from front to back and

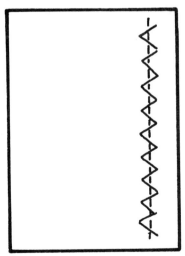

Fig. 8.16 To create the look of hand piecing, zigzag over a seam of straight stitches. Then press the seam open.

tie a knot at the end. Zigzag stitch over the thread, pulling on it gently as you stitch.

Imitating hand piecing on quilts

Here is a seam shown to me by a quilter. After stitching two quilt pieces together, run a narrow zigzag over this line of straight stitches (Fig. 8.16). When the seam is pressed open, it gives the impression of perfect hand piecing. Why not skip the first step of straight stitching? Because the two passes will make the quilt seams sturdier, and the line of straight stitching is an excellent guideline for the zigzagging.

Joining veiling with a scallop stitch

What kind of a seam can be used on veiling? In Lesson 17, a straight seam is stitched on Alençon lace, using a close zigzag stitch. A more decorative seam is stitched with the built-in scallop stitch. Overlap the edges, stitch, then cut back excess material on each side to the scallop.

Using built-in stitches

Don't overlook the built-in jersey and honeycomb stitches on your machine. They are sewn from the top of the fabric. You may have avoided using them when sewing ribbing onto sweatshirts or for top decoration if you experimented on thick fabric and had an uneven look to your stitches. But now you can balance the stitches on many machines. Using a sample of the same fabrics, use the balance pushbuttons (+ and −) to find the correct setting for a perfect decorative stitch.

Built-in stitches can be sewn between two pieces of fabric to create an open, interesting seam (Fig. 8.17). The gathering stitch on many machines is one that works beautifully, as does the feather stitch. The feather stitch is one of my favorites. I use it on quilt tops to stitch the layers together.

I also used the gathering stitch on a Ber-

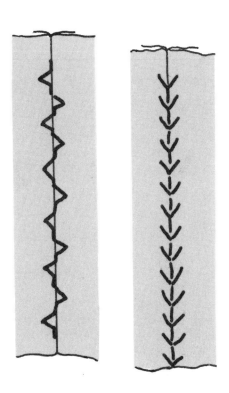

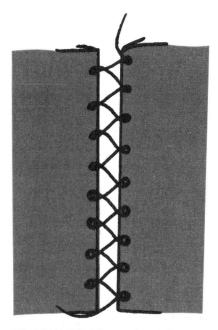

Fig. 8.18 Stitching a decorative seam using free machining.

Fig. 8.17 (left) Decorate and stitch a seam with either the gathering stitch (left) or feather stitch.

muda bag I made from Ultrasuede scraps. Using a commercial kit, I cut the scraps into squares and rectangles—enough to cover the pattern. I used the Teflon presser foot and polyester thread to stitch the scraps together. To do this, I lifted them in pairs from the pattern and sewed the horizontal seams first. Then I went back and sewed the vertical seams. When the stitching was completed, I placed the pattern over the Ultrasuede and cut off fabric projecting beyond the edges. After that, I was able to finish the bag according to the kit directions.

Creating seams with feed dogs lowered

If you use a similar seam with fabric instead of Ultrasuede, fold under seam allowances at least 5/8″ (15.9mm) and press.

Move the two pieces of fabric about 1/8″ (3.2mm) apart, topsides down. If the fabric is washable, you may want to slip water-soluble stabilizer under it and baste the fabric 1/8″ apart. Use thick cord in the bobbin. Lower the feed dogs and use the darning foot. Sew freely from one side of the fabric to the other, making loops as you enter and leave it (Fig. 8.18). When you finish, turn it over and stitch down along the folds again. Then cut back underneath to the stitching.

These techniques only scratch the surface of interesting seams for your fabric. New seams are introduced every time a new utility or decorative stitch is incorporated into a machine. They are welcome, of course, but in the meantime there is no lack of beautiful and practical work you can do.

CHAPTER 9

Adding Hems and Edges

I remember when "good clothes" didn't mean "clean jeans." There were puffed sleeves, sweetheart necklines—always braided, piped, or embroidered in some way. We wanted to dress like movie stars. Dresses were molded to them and then decorated creatively. Designers always took many long-cuts.

The more you know about your machine, the more inventive you can become: no more boring clothes! You may not think you'll ever use all the decorative hems and edgings in this chapter, but make samples for your notebook anyway. You may be surprised.

With the range of fabrics and styles now available, and the variety of effects we want to achieve, choosing the appropriate hem or edge is not always easy. Before sewing a hem or decorative edge on anything, ask yourself these questions: What type of fabric? What type of garment? Who is the garment for? Will it be worn forever? How decorative is it to be?

I have my favorite ways to hem and finish edges. I've also learned hems and edges I will never do again. What makes the difference? Appearance, of course, and ease of stitching. I think I have tried every imaginable variation, and those that follow are the ones I prefer because they are useful and good-looking.

Stitch samples of each and put the results in your notebook for reference. Include your own favorites as well. Write the machine settings on each one, along with comments such as what fabrics work well, where you would use them, whether they were long-cuts with happy endings or more trouble than they were worth.

Lesson 25. Turning hems once

I used to cringe at the thought of hems turned only once—all those raw edges! But I have changed my way of thinking.

Using double needles on knits

My favorite hem for T-shirts and other casual knits is turned once and stitched in place with a double needle. The two stitching lines share one bobbin thread, giving the stitches the stretch they need.

Stitch width: 0
Stitch length: 2
Needle position: center
Needle: double, at least 2mm
Tension: *top,* normal; *bobbin,* normal
Fabric: knit
Presser foot: pintuck or embroidery foot
Thread: polyester
Stabilizer: tear-away

It is simple to fold up the hem and sew with a double needle from the topside of the fabric.

When finished, trim the fabric back to the stitching underneath. The sewn-out zigzag can be used for variation. Handwalk the needle through the first few stitches to be sure the zigzag will clear the needle plate opening.

Hemming with a double needle on sheers

Use a double needle for sheer fabrics, too. When a narrow hem would be neither suitable nor attractive, fold up a 4″ (10.2cm) hem on lightweight fabrics and sew across. Lightweight garments hang better with the weight of a deep hem and it's also more attractive when the hem of the underskirt isn't visible underneath.

Of course you can add more rows of stitching, evenly spaced from the first. Cut back to the top of the stitching.

Hemming with built-in stitches on front

The next hem for delicate fabrics is much the same, but uses a single needle and the built-in scallop stitch.

Stitch width: 4
Stitch length: 1/2
Needle position: center
Presser foot: embroidery foot

To hem heavy, canvas-type fabrics with

a machine that will do a triple straight or zigzag stitch, first find the correct width and length by practicing on a piece of the same fabric you will use for the finished article. Set up the machine for a triple zigzag or straight stitch.

Stitch width: varies
Stitch length: varies
Needle position: center
Needle: #110 jeans
Presser foot: special purpose foot (reverse action)

This is an extremely strong stitch. Use it for anything from deck furniture canvas to jeans.

Refer back to the stitch samples you did in Chapter 2. You may prefer other decora-

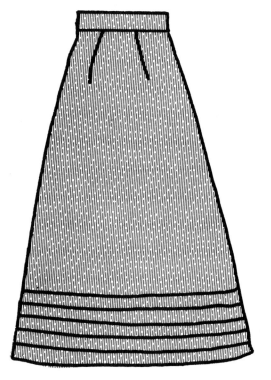

Fig. 9.1 Use light flannel between hem and skirt, then quilt the hem with lines of straight stitching.

tive built-in stitches to those mentioned here. Experiment with different fabrics and built-in stitches, keeping all your samples in your notebook.

Quilting a hem

Another single-fold hem can be done on heavy materials such as wool or velveteen. Use a walking foot. Allow about 8" (20.3cm) for the hem of the skirt. Put light batting, such as flannel sheeting, inside and pin in place. Sew four or five rows of straight stitches, one line at a time, to quilt the hem (Fig. 9.1). Space the lines of stitching as you wish. Try quilting a long Christmas skirt or an evening skirt using metallic thread.

Or turn the skirt inside out and put pearl cotton on the bobbin to contrast with the skirt. The topside will be against the bed of the machine. Stitch rows, then cut back to the last line of stitching. This can be done around sleeve bands or down jacket facings as well.

Lesson 26. Blind hemming

I remember when most of the hems I put in garments were blind hems worked by hand. Times have changed, but that doesn't mean I've given up blind hems. The only difference is that I do them more quickly now—by machine.

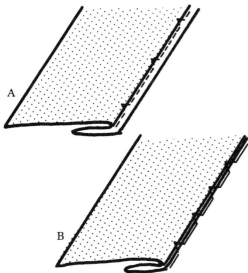

Fig. 9.2 Blind hemming. A. Fold over the hem, then fold the skirt back, letting 1/8" (3.2mm) show beyond the edge; stitch on the edge of the fabric. B. Or fold the garment back even with the edge, and stitch off the fabric, the left swing stitching the fold.

Stitch width: 2 1/4 – 2 1/2
Stitch length: 2
Needle position: right
Feed dogs: up
Presser foot: blind stitch
Built-in stitch: blind hem
Tension: *top,* loosened; *bobbin,* normal
Thread: sewing
Accessories: dressmakers' pins

To begin the hem, decide first if you can live with a raw edge. If you can, then leave it as it is, but if you hate that unfinished edge, then attach a lace edging over it or stitch around the edge with the sewn-out zigzag stitch before you proceed.

Turn up the hem 1½" to 2" (3.8cm to 5.1cm) and pin very closely around it, about an inch from the top. If the fabric slips, the hem will be a mess, so don't try to save time by not pinning a lot.

Or use Tami Durand's method. Baste the hem and skirt together, by machine, ¼" from the edge of the turned-up hem. There will definitely be no slipping. Fold back and proceed as you do with the pinned hem. When finished, pull out the basting.

Set your machine up.

Fold the garment back on itself, leaving

⅛" (3.2mm) of hem at the edge to stitch on (Fig. 9.2A). Put the fold of the fabric against the left side of the black middle extension or place the fabric inside the extension of the blind stitch foot (refer to your manual). Stitch on the edge of the fabric and let the needle catch about 2 threads of the fold. Check the settings on scrap fabric first to determine the correct stitch width and length. Thick fabrics will require different settings than lightweight fabrics.

I made a fine batiste bishop dress with yards of blind hemming, but the stitching pulled too tightly. Despite the fine thread, loosened tension, and a #60 needle, I didn't like the looks of it. The answer? I sewed from off the fabric. I folded the fabric back so the fold met the edge exactly. Then I stitched outside the fabric and the left bite held it together with no pulling (Fig. 9.2B). I've tried it on several heavier weights of fabric as well, and it works beautifully.

Still hesitant about stitching in space? Then place water-soluble stabilizer under your stitching.

Lesson 27. Sewing narrow hems

Next to hemstitching needles, the most unused accessories are the hemming presser feet. I think I know why: few stitchers ever take time to practice with them. They're great time savers, but I had to learn to use them, too. Now after yards of hem samples, I can't do without them.

Set up your machine, read the directions, and reread as you work. Before you begin to hem a garment with one of the hemmers, cut back the seam allowances that have to be sewn over. Then learn to start the fabric. I hated starting a hem because of those first problem inches until I tried Gail Brown's method, which follows.

Straight stitching

Practice with a medium-width hemmer at first, because it is easier to use when learning. Also needed are lightweight cotton to hem and a 3" (7.6cm) square of tear-away stabilizer.

Overlap the piece of tear-away stabilizer with the fabric about ¼" (6.3mm) and sew them together. Start rolling the stabilizer into the scroll of the hemming foot. By the time the fabric is introduced into the hemmer, the hem is being sewn down starting on the first thread of the fabric.

Guide the fabric by holding it taut and lifting it slightly as it rolls through the foot. The edge of the fabric must be vertical. As long as you pay attention, guiding and holding the fabric correctly, the machine does the rest.

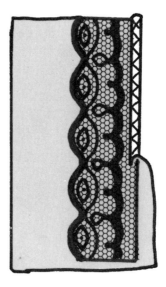

Fig. 9.3 Lace is attached with a finished edge in one step.

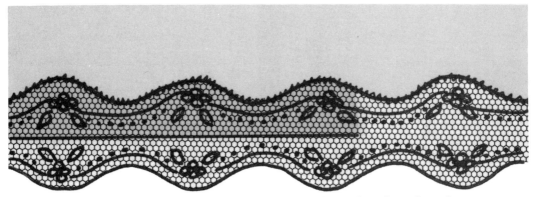

Fig. 9.4 Attach scalloped lace to fabric by overlapping it, zigzagging along the scalloped edge, then cutting the fabric back to the stitching line.

Sewing on lace

This method is simple and it does save time.

Stitch width: 3−4
Stitch length: 1−1 1/2
Needle position: left
Presser foot: buttonhole, appliqué, invisible zipper foot or open embroidery
Fabric: lightweight cotton, lace edging
Thread: fine sewing thread to match

Place the lace on top of the fabric, topsides together, the edge of the lace ⅛″ (6.3mm) from the edge of the fabric.

The fabric is usually placed to the right of the middle of the presser foot but practice first with the presser foot you choose. As you sew, it will roll and be whipped over the heading of the lace (Fig. 9.3).

See other methods of sewing lace to fabric in Lesson 25, "French handsewing."

Attaching scalloped lace

Apply scalloped lace to fabric, topsides up, by overlapping it to make a hem (Fig. 9.4). Let the fabric extend well past the curve on top of the lace. Baste lace to fabric. Zigzag along the edge, following the scallop. Cut back the fabric underneath to the stitching line.

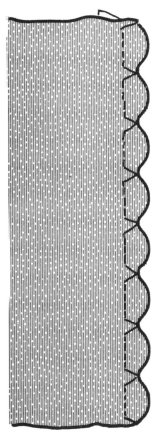

Fig. 9.5 A shell edge on tricot, stitched with the blindhem stitch.

123

Fig. 9.6 Roll and shell edges are used for decorative hems on lingerie fabrics.

Stitching shell edging

This is a good hem and edging for lingerie (Fig. 9.5). Or use it to decorate ribbon and tucks.

Set up your machine:

Stitch width: 4
Stitch length: 1
Needle position: center
Feed dogs: up
Presser foot: zigzag
Built-in stitch: blind hem pattern

If you are going to cross a seam when hemming, then cut back the seam allowances that will be sewn over.

The foot rests on the fabric for this one; you do not feed fabric into the foot. Fold the fabric under ½″ (12.7mm) and place the folded edge to the left. Stitch, letting the left swing of the needle sew over the edge, creating the shell pattern. At the end, cut back to the stitching underneath.

Roll and shell hemming

The roll and shell hemmer (accommodates a zigzag stitch) not only makes a narrow, straight-stitch hem, but it also rolls and shells as shown in Fig. 9.6, if the machine is set on zigzag. Usually it's the finish of choice when hemming tricot, as it decorates and hems in one operation. It's impossible to turn square corners on these hems, so round off any corners before you begin to stitch. Because tricot rolls to one side, hem with the right side up. If you will stitch over a seam while hemming, first cut back the seam allowances you'll cross so the fabric will feed in without a problem. As the fabric is rolled into the foot, it will curl and be sewn into a narrow, puffy roll.

Stitch width: 4
Stitch length: 2 1/2
Needle position: center
Feed dogs: up
Presser foot: roll-and-shell hemmer

It's important to keep the fabric straight ahead of the presser foot and raise it a bit to keep it feeding easily. The needle goes into the fabric at the left, then off the edge of the fabric at the right.

Lesson 28. Using bias tape

I must admit, I equate bias tape with the edges of Grandma's apron, but now that I can apply it so easily, I'm finding new ways to use it. I especially like it for toddlers' sunsuits and dresses.

This is the only method I use; what I like best about it is that the tape is sewn on almost invisibly. You don't need the bias binder accessory.

Look at the bias tape: One side is wider than the other. The wide side will be on the back of your work. Open the bias tape and place the narrow side on top, the cut edge of the tape along the cut edge of the fabric. If there is a ⅝″ (15.9mm) seam, cut it back to fit the width of the bias. Pin in place.

Adjust the foot or needle position—it will depend upon the foot you use—and the fabric will either be held against the side of the foot or a middle extension will ride on the crease to ensure a perfect stitch-in-the-ditch. Stitch along the crease.

Fold the tape over the edge. I sometimes dab the underside with glue stick between

> Stitch width: 0
> Stitch length: 2
> Feed dogs: up
> Presser foot: edging or blind hem foot
> Needle: #80
> Needle position: center
> Thread: monofilament
> Fabric: lightweight cotton, double-fold bias tape
> Accessories: glue stick, pins

tape and fabric. Pin if you wish, or baste by hand.

Press the bias and check that the underside of the bias extends slightly beyond the seam line on the topside.

From the topside, stitch in the ditch of the seam. Again, adjust the foot to enable you to sew exactly in the ditch. The stitching catches the edge of the bias underneath. I've decided I can't sew without the edging foot.

Lesson 29. Zigzagging a narrow edge

This is only one of several methods to produce a strong, finished hem or edge of tiny, tight zigzag stitches. Use it to finish ruffles, napkins and scarves.

Fold the fabric under about ½″ (12.7mm) and guide the fold of the fabric

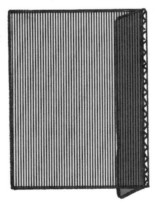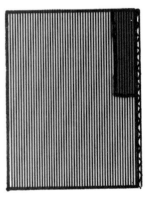

Fig. 9.7 From the top of the fabric, sew a narrow, close zigzag down the folded edge (left). Cut back the fabric underneath to the stitching line.

exactly in the middle of the embroidery foot (I often use the hole in the #030 Bernina foot for a guide).

Look through your presser feet and find one marked or grooved to use as a guide. Be sure it will accommodate satin stitches. Stitch on the fabric with the left swing of the needle, the right swing stitching just off the right side of it (Fig. 9.7). After stitching is completed, cut the fabric back to the stitched edge, as partially done below.

Lesson 30. Covering wire for shaped edges

In a bridal shop I saw yard goods that included nylon filament at the edges of chiffon and organdy ruffles. It was an attractive finish for the ruffles that can be applied to skirt and sleeve hems or across the drop-shoulders of wedding gowns and formal wear.

A case displayed dozens of headpieces using the same nylon filament to keep bows perky and ribbons from wilting. You are invited to create your own, combining filament and sheer fabrics, beads and silk flowers.

I could also see many Halloween costume possibilities here. Use the filament at the bottom edge of a long, filmy skirt or, if you want to make an angel costume, use heavy gauge filament for floppy wings.

Nylon filament is available by the yard at stores that sell bridal lace and fabrics. But I found that it is much easier to buy 25-pound-test fishing line in a sporting goods store. Cheaper, too. I've used both and I don't think there's a difference. There are different weights to fishing lines, which means they come in different thicknesses.

For super-thick costume fabric, you can use weed-trimmer line. It comes in a 50-foot length and the diameter to use is .05mm. This fits in the groove of the non-automatic Bernina buttonhole foot. Use the same foot or experiment with a double-grooved foot in your supplies. Use the

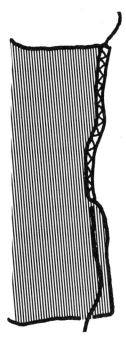

Fig. 9.8 Rolling fabric over nylon filament or wire creates a rigid, finished edge.

same method to apply any of the nylon filament mentioned.

I've used appliqué and pintuck feet also. The settings will be different, so experiment with needle positions.

I placed the filament about ¼" (6.3mm) from the edge of the fabric (the needle should stitch off the edge of the material on the right swing). As you sew, the edge of the fabric will roll over and enclose the line (Fig. 9.8).

Milliner's wire or florist's wire is available already covered with thread. Both of these can be stitched into the edge of fabric in the same way as nylon filament. They both come in different gauges. Unlike the nylon edge, the wire can be bent into any shape you might want. Buy milliner's wire at bridal shops and florist's wire at craft shops. Make flower petals and leaves using wire.

Lesson 31. Cording edges

Covering cords

Covered cord produces one of the finest, prettiest edges to use on table linens, on scarves, collars, wherever you want a delicate but very strong edge.

Fold the fabric under about ½" (12.7mm) and press. Thread pearl cotton through the hole in the cording foot. Place

> Stitch width: 2, 4
> Stitch length: 1/2
> Needle position: center
> Presser foot: cording foot or foot that has slot to guide cord, such as non-automatic Bernina button hole foot
> Thread: machine-embroidery or sewing thread; #5 pearl cotton

the hole at the edge of the fabric and stitch (Fig. 9.9). Cut back to the stitching underneath when it's completed.

To create a thicker edge, go back over the first line of stitching with the Bernina non-automatic buttonhole foot. Place the edge you've completed in the slot to the left and another cord of pearl cotton between the toes of the presser foot to hold it in place. Change to stitch width 4.

If you use this method to finish the edge of a collar, you won't need to turn the collar. Instead, sew with wrong sides of upper and under collar together to eliminate the bulk of a turned-in seam allowance.

To make a delicate edging for a bridal veil, cord the edge.

> Stitch width: 2
> Stitch length: 1/2 – 3/4 (not too tight)
> Needle position: center
> Presser foot: cording foot

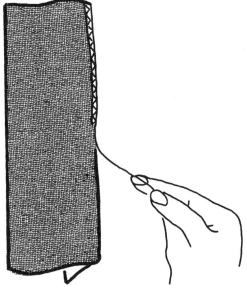

Fig. 9.9 Zigzagging over cord produces a strong corded edge.

127

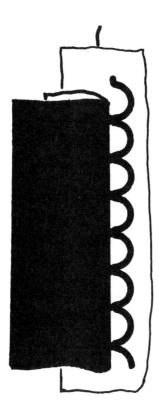

Fig. 9.10 Make a crocheted edge with the built-in scallop stitch.

Thread: fine sewing thread to match veil; #8 pearl cotton to match veil

Without folding the veiling, place it so the edge extends past the presser foot on the right. Slip #8 pearl cotton in the hole of the cording foot. Sew over the pearl. Cut back to the pearl for a fine finished edge. (Try a corded scallop stitch, too.)

Creating crocheted edges

This decorative edge is used to finish shirt plackets and collars. It's a delicate, lacelike finish that lends itself to feminine clothes and baby items.

Instead of threading pearl cotton or gimp through the presser foot, this time it is threaded up through the needle plate on the bed of the machine.

Stitch width: 4
Stitch length: almost 0
Presser foot: cording foot
Built-in stitch: scallop
Fabric: medium-weight cotton
Thread: color to contrast with fabric; gimp or #5 pearl cotton the same color as the thread
Accessories: tear-away stabilizer or colored paper to match thread

Use the cording foot and pearl cotton to do a corded edge using the scallop stitch. Place stabilizer underneath and far enough to the right to be under the stitch-

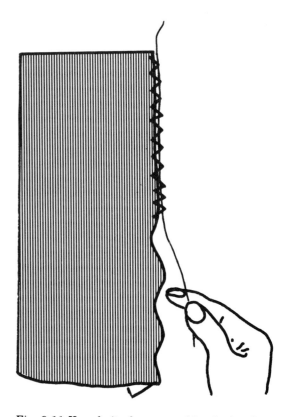

Fig. 9.11 Keep knits from stretching by stitching in an elastic thread.

es, as shown in Fig. 9.10. The fabric should be doubled; the fold is placed just to the left of the hole in front of the presser foot. Stitch at the edge. The scallops will catch the fabric, but most of the stitches will be off the edge onto the stabilizer (Fig. 9.10). Carefully tear off the stabilizer when you finish.

Try other decorative stitches at the edges of fabrics. I like the small, undulating scallop, too. Use it on the edges of plackets or sleeves and decorate collars with it. Sew on doubled fabric, then cut back to the stitching. The edge of the baby bonnet in Fig. 5.10 was worked this way.

Reshaping knits with elastic

Elastic can be used to keep stretchy edges in shape, or to reshape them.

Stitch width: 2
Stitch length: 2 or your preference
Presser foot: cording foot

Thread the elastic though the hole in the cording foot. Keep the elastic at the edge of the knit and sew down the fold (Fig. 9.11).

Lesson 32. Making thread fringe

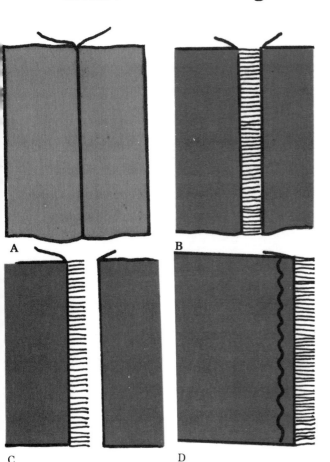

A

B

C

D

Stitch width: 2
Stitch length: almost 0
Presser foot: tailor tacking
Thread: machine-embroidery
Fabric: medium-weight cotton
Stabilizer: tear-away

How many machine owners use a tailor-tacking foot for tailor tacking? I can't find one. Most of the time the tailor tacking foot is used for fringing (Fig. 9.12), fagoting, or for sewing on buttons.

To make a fringed edge, you will need two pieces of fabric. Both pieces will be folded under about ⅝" (15.9mm), but one piece of fabric will be eliminated later.

Loosen the top tension. I think it is more successful to take the thread out of the tension slot altogether if it is possible with your machine.

Fig. 9.12 Making thread fringe. A. Butt two pieces of fabric together. Stitch down between folds with zigzag stitches over the tailor-tacking foot. B. Open up the stitching and pull out the bobbin thread. C. Then pull off one side of fabric. D. Use a decorative stitch to sew along the fringed edge.

129

Don't overlap, but butt the fabric folds next to each other. Hold them together as you sew down between them (Fig. 9.12A). Pull the bobbin thread out, then *very carefully* pull the fabrics apart, but leave them connected by the stitching (Fig. 9.12B). Care can make or break your work as the fringe wants to jump out of the fabric until you accomplish the next step.

Put the thread back into tension and place a stabilizer under the fabric. You may also want to put a stabilizer on top of the fringe to keep it from catching on the presser foot. On the side that will retain the fringe, stitch a line of decorative stitches along the fold to keep the fringe in place. Carefully pull off the other piece of fabric (Fig. 9.12C, D)

If you look closely at the eyelashes of the denim doll in Fig. 3.17, you will see thread fringe. As you get to know your machine, you'll see more and more ways to use it to make the simplest tasks even simpler. On to the next lesson.

Lesson 33. Piping edges

Miniature piping is especially pretty and colorful on the edges of children's clothing. Use a #3 or #5 pearl cotton and a piece of bias fabric twice the width of the seam allowance. I may not use bias fabric at all. It seems to make little difference, and though held sacrilegious, you can save fabric by cutting on the straight, so try it for yourself. Or cover the pearl with purchased bias tape.

Use a presser foot with a narrow groove: either pintuck, invisible zipper foot, or appliqué foot. Each has a groove in which to fit the covered pearl while stitching it. Adjust the needle position to sew at the edge of the cord.

To cover thick cord for upholstery, use a Bernina bulky overlock foot or one comparable for your machine. Forget what you've learned about always using a zipper foot for this procedure. The wrapped cord fits into the groove of the overlock foot and never slips. I sewed over 100 yards of that one day and it couldn't have been easier. Attaching covered cording to a pillow is also a breeze with this foot.

Lesson 34. Topstitching

There is nothing richer-looking on a coat or suit than an even line of topstitching.

When you need a narrowly spaced double line, use a double needle. For topstitching a heavy fabric, I use a topstitching needle with two sewing threads, eliminating the fraying of buttonhole twist. Sew the second line of stitching in the same direction as the first.

When topstitching on lapels, the roll line indicates where the top threads will go to the underside. For this reason, if you use two threads on top, you must use two threads on the bobbin as well. Wind the bobbin with two threads at one time instead of using only one. Then treat the threads as if they were one.

Instead of anchoring threads, leave a long enough thread at the beginning and the end to work in later invisibly by hand.

If you have a machine that will triple straight stitch, experiment. Use orange thread to stitch on denim seams to duplicate the look of commercial topstitching on jeans.

How can you keep topstitching straight?

You have several choices. Use tape along the edge of the fabric and sew next to it. Use the Cut'n'Sew accessory (width is limited). Again, using the edging foot is my first choice because the width can be set with needle positioning.

If using lightweight material, set the machine for 10 – 12 stitches per inch. If using medium-weight fabric, a longer stitch looks better. Stitch samples on scraps of the same material to see what stitch length setting you prefer.

I think there is hope for more decorative dressing. Have you noticed how Joan Crawford's clothes don't look so funny anymore?

CHAPTER **10**

Machine Tricks: Adding Threads to Threads

- **Lesson 35. Making cord**
- **Lesson 36. Making tassels**

For nine chapters, we've used fabric and thread for sewing and embroidering. I'll bet you know your sewing machine pretty well by now, but there's more: In this chapter, I'll show you how to make cords using your machine. Some will be used for practical purposes, such as belt loops and hangers for pendants, but we'll make other cords for decoration, bunching them together into tassels.

Lesson 35. Making cord

Twisting monk's cord

Monk's cord is made from several strands of thread or yarn held together and twisted to make a thick cord. The cord may be used in many ways—as a finish around pillows, as a handle for handbags, and as thick fringe in tassels.

On the machine, monk's cord is made using the bobbin winder. If your bobbin has holes in the top of it, tie the cord onto it through one of the holes. If your bobbin is all metal or all plastic without a hole, the cord size is limited, as you will slip the cord down through the center of the bobbin and seat the bobbin on the winder. Pearl cotton (#8) is the thickest that will seat properly. (However, there is a way to get around this. You can tie dental floss—it doesn't slip—around the center of a thick cord, leaving long enough ends to seat the floss into the middle of the bobbin winder. Then you are able to wind monk's cord of any thickness.)

If you are working alone, you will also be

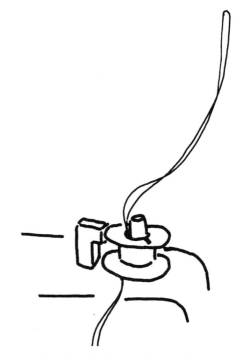

Fig. 10.1 Make monk's cord by slipping a doubled pearl cotton thread down inside the bobbin and activating the bobbin winder.

Fig. 10.2 Machine-made
monk's cord is used to make
this tassel.

the cord with your other hand. Hold onto that spot while you place the loop from your finger over the thread holder pin, if it is close enough. Otherwise, keeping tension on the cord, bring both ends together and very carefully let it twist to make a monk's cord. Work down the twists with both hands to keep the cord smooth. At this point you will see that it is more successful if you work with a partner.

When the cord is twisted as tightly as it will go, take it out of the bobbin and off the thread-holder spool pin. Tie an overhand knot to hold the ends together until you actually use it.

I use this cord to make thick fringe for tassels, sometimes slipping washers, bells,

limited by the length of cord you can use and still reach the machine's foot pedal. Use a 2 yard (1.7m) length. Fold this in half, knot the two ends together, and slip the knot down through the center of a bobbin. Or thread one end through one of the bobbin holes, bring the two ends together, and tie. Of course you can tie the cord onto the bobbin through one of the holes and work with one cord, not two. If you do work with one cord, tie a loop at the end of the cord to slip your finger through before you begin to twist the cord.

Next, push the bobbin down into place on the pin (Fig. 10.1). When clicked into place, the bobbin will hold the cord securely. Put your index finger in the loop of cord at the other end and stretch the cord to keep tension on it. Activate the bobbin mechanism.

Keep winding the cord until it is so tight the blood supply to your finger is threatened. Work your finger out of the loop and, still holding it tightly, find the middle of

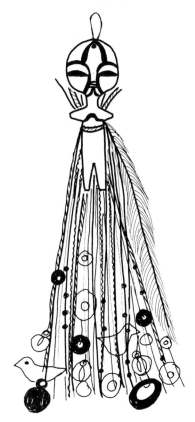

Fig. 10.3 A doll tassel made
with monk's cord.

beads or a spacer to the middle of the cord after I have twisted it and before I double it and make the final twists (Figs. 10.2 and 10.3).

These quick cords can be used for belt loops, button loops, ties for clothing. Or twist up a batch to tie small packages.

Stitching belt and button loops

Belt loop cords can be made by pulling out the bobbin and top threads and folding them over to make about six strands. Use a stitch width 4 and water-soluble stabilizer underneath if your machine will not sew without it. Set your machine for free machining, with feed dogs down or covered. Use a darning foot or no presser foot at all. Hold the threads tightly, front and back, as you stitch. You will feed the threads under the needle and determine the stitch length. These tiny cords work well for corded buttonholes.

You can also zigzag over thicker cords and hold them together. If you add a contrasting thread color, you can make interesting tassels (see the next lesson).

Lesson 36. Making tassels

I'm drawn to tassels. I sketch them when I see them in museums or books, and I have a notebook full of ideas cut from magazines. I've labored over a few myself, using hand embroidery, even tiny macramé knots. Sometimes they look like fetish dolls—another weakness—and so I play them that way.

How can my sewing machine help me make tassels? First of all, I make monk's cord using the bobbin winder. I combine those with other cords, sometimes stringing beads or bells on them (Figs. 10.4 and 10.5).

I can also use a braiding foot or open embroidery foot to make colorful cord. Holding several pearl cotton cords together, I place them in the groove on the bottom of the presser foot and zigzag stitch over the pearl with a contrasting color. I choose a stitch width 4 to enclose the cords, and a stitch length 1 to let some of the cord show through.

Project
Tassel Collar

Several ways to make tassels by machine involve using water-soluble stabilizer. The first method is for a collar of stitched cords to wrap around the main tassel cords.

First fold the 16″ (40.6cm) lengths of

Stitch width: 4
Stitch length: 1/2
Needle position: center
Needle: #80
Presser foot: open embroidery
Feed dogs: up
Tension: *top*, normal; *bobbin*, normal
Cord: 16 yards (14m) rayon cord (available at fabric shops) for the collar; #5 pearl cotton to match cord; many yards of string, thread or yarn for main part of tassel (the more yarn used, the plumper and more attractive the tassel), cut into 16″ (40.6cm) lengths
Thread: rayon embroidery to match rayon cord
Accessories: water-soluble stabilizer

---

yarn in half to find their centers. Use one yarn piece to tie the lengths together there. Knot tightly. Then tie an overhand knot with the ends of that cord to make a hanger for the tassel.

Cut six dozen 8″ (20.3cm) lengths of pur-

Fig. 10.5 More tassels stitched by machine.

Fig. 10.4 Monk's cord is used for the tassels at left and center. A collar, stitched by machine, was used for the one at right.

chased rayon cord. Place a piece of water-soluble stabilizer on the bed of the machine and lay these cords next to each other across the stabilizer (in horizontal rows as you are looking at them). Starting ½″ (12.7mm) in from the right side, place a strand of #5 pearl cotton perpendicular to and crossing all the cords (Fig. 10.6). Satin

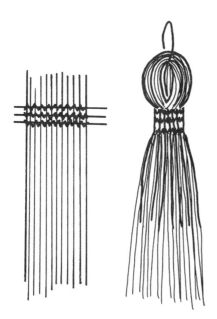

Fig. 10.6 Make a collar for the tassel by placing cords next to each other, then zigzagging over cords laid at right angles across them.

Project
Covered Wire
Tassel

Cover 18″ (45.7cm) of milliner's wire with stitches for the next tassel (Fig. 10.7).

Set up your machine and place water-soluble stabilizer under the wire if you wish. Sew over the wire. If the wire doesn't feed well, then use a longer length stitch and go over it twice. The milliner's wire is covered with thread and this keeps the rayon stitches from slipping.

Make 45 thick cords for the tassel by zigzagging over two 12″ (30.5cm) strands of #5 pearl cotton for each one. *Hint:* Stitch two 15-yard-long (14m-long) cords together and cut them into 12″ (30.5cm) pieces.

To use the wire for the tassel, first fold the 12″ (30.5cm) long cords in half. Slip an end of the wire through the fold, extending it past the cord 2″ (5.1cm). Bend the wire back 1″ (2.5cm) at the end and twist it around itself to make a loop for hanging (the loop will enclose the cords).

With the other end of the wire, wrap the tassel around and around till you reach halfway down the length of it. Hold the end of the wire with the tweezers. Wrap it around the point of the tweezers to make a decorative coil at the end (Fig. 10.7).

stitch over the pearl cotton and the rayon cords. Sew down several more rows of pearl, lining up each pearl cord next to the one stitched before it. When completed, cut off the ½″ (12.7mm) rayon threads protruding from the top of the collar. Zigzag over the edge, which will give the top a smooth finish.

Wrap the collar, inside-out, 1½″ (3.8cm) down from the fold of the tassel cords. Pin the collar tightly around the cords. Remove it from the tassel and machine stitch the ends of the collar together. Cut back to the stitching line and zigzag over the edge. Turn right side out, then pull the yarn tassel cords from the bottom through the collar to complete it. The collar should fit snugly.

You could embroider the same basic collar in an almost endless variety of ways for your tassel collection.

Stitch width: 4
Stitch length: 1/2
Needle position: center
Needle: #80
Feed dogs: up
Presser foot: open embroidery foot
Tension: *top,* normal; *bobbin,* normal
Thread: rayon embroidery
Accessories: tweezers
Stabilizer: water-soluble (optional),
    cut into long strips 1″ wide

Fig. 10.7 Cover milliner's wire with stitches and twist the wire around cords to make a tassel.

Project
Doll Tassel

The fertility doll tassel is a combination of several dozen 10″ (25.4cm) cords, including linen, jute and monk's cords (see Fig. 10.3) all tied to a small African doll. I placed the bundle of cords on the bed of the machine, letting it extend 1″ (2.5cm) to the right of the presser foot and flattening it with my fingers to allow me to stitch over the cords. The machine was set up for free-machining, with feed dogs lowered and a darning foot in place. Using the widest zig-zag, I stitched forward and back across the cords. When I finished, I spread glue from a glue stick across the stitching on one side of the bundle and placed this at the back of the doll, wrapping and tying it in place with a linen cord.

To decorate the tassel, I slipped a long feather under the linen wrapping cord, and strung some of the tassel cords with beads, brass bells and metal washers. Overhand knots held the objects in place at different heights on the cords. There's a hole in the top of the doll, so I added a loop of cord there to hang the tassel.

Project
Making
Two Tassel Tops
by Machine

For the following tassels shown in Fig. 10.8C and 10.9, the tops are made on the sewing machine. Put a 7″ (17.8cm) square of felt in a 5″ (12.7cm) spring hoop. Draw half a circle and embroider this using decorative, built-in machine stitches. Take it out of the hoop and cut out the half-circle (Fig. 10.8A). Cut out a wedge from the side

Stitch width: widest
Stitch length: varies
Needle position: center
Needle: #90, topstitch
Feed dogs: up
Presser foot: overlock, cording, or pintuck foot; embroidery foot
Tension: *top,* loosened; *bobbin,* normal
Fabric suggestion: 9″ (22.9cm) square of felt (tassel top will be completely covered with stitches)
Thread: rayon machine embroidery–I chose red, yellow and blue; #8 red pearl cotton; #5 blue pearl cotton (optional)
Accessories: 7″ (17.8cm) spring hoop, small bells, glue stick, fine-point marker
Stabilizer: tear-away

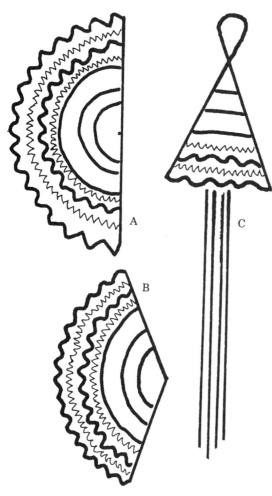

together at the middle with a cord 8″ (20.3cm) long. Thread that cord through a large-eyed needle and push it up from inside through the top of the cone. Tie a knot at the end and hang the tassel.

The second tassel is also made of felt, with a machine-stitched top (Fig. 10.9).

The finished size of the tassel top is 2″ × 2″ (5.1cm × 5.1cm). I worked with a 9″ (22.9cm) piece of felt so it would fit in the

Fig. 10.8 Making a machined tassel. A. Embroider a half-circle of felt. B. Cut a wedge from it, and sew up the sides to form a cone. C. The cone becomes the top of the tassel.

of the half-circle (Fig. 10.8B). Fold the larger piece in half, topsides together. Straight stitch the cut edges. Turn to the right side.

Cut six tassel cords, each 18″ (45.7cm) in length, from rayon cord or machine-made monk's cord. Find the center and tie them

Fig. 10.9 A tassel made of satin stitches on felt.

138

7" (17.8cm) spring hoop. This allows enough room for the presser foot without hitting the edge of the hoop, as you will stitch both sides of the tassel top—2" × 4" (30.5cm × 10.2cm) area—at once.

Trace the pattern from Fig. 10.9. Cut around the tracing and lay this on the felt. Draw around the pattern with a marker (it won't show when tassel is completed).

Begin by carefully stretching the felt in the hoop. Use the overlock foot for this top or use corded (#5 pearl cotton) satin stitches with the cording or pintuck foot. Starting on the right side, place one line of close, smooth satin stitches. Add another row next to the first, and continue, changing colors as you wish. Now sew between the satin stitches, using a contrasting color and the triple stitch if your machine has one built in. If it doesn't, you can also use double thread in a topstitching needle, with a straight stitch.

Cut out the stitched design; then cut it in half. Place wrong sides together.

Cut about five dozen lengths of pearl cotton, each 12" (30.5cm) long. Fold them in half. Place the folds inside the felt pieces along the straight edge. Pin the felt together or use a dot of glue stick to hold everything in place as you stitch. Zigzag across the straight edge of the felt to keep the pearl cotton in place. Zigzag around the curve as well. Then go back with a satin stitch and stitch around it again with stitch width at the widest, stitch length 1/2. Add bells to each side and a hanger at the top. Clay or metal found objects also work well as ornaments.

I agree, making tassels is a nutty thing to do (but it's fun). Use them to decorate your tote bag, for key chains, zipper pulls, decorations on clothing, curtain tiebacks. I confess that I hang them all over my sewing room.

CHAPTER 11

Decorative Stitches

- **Lesson 37. Decorating with stitches**
- **Lesson 38. Sewing techniques using decorative stitches**
- **Lesson 39. Using machine accessories with decorative stitches**

In addition to zigzag and blind hem, many machines today also contain other utility stitches, like stretch stitch for knits, and several decorative stitches, like the scallop and feather stitches. The fancier the machine, the more stitches. The new computer machines allow you to write messages and to combine decorative stitches. Some even allow you to graph and program your own creations! But despite all the variety, these stitches are too often not used at all, for lack of ideas. (By the way, many of the names of built-in stitches differ from one machine to another, so refer to your man-

ual and also look at the illustrations if the names I mention sound foreign to you.)

This chapter is divided into three lessons. The first contains ideas for stitching rows of decoration or stitching single motifs. Lesson 38 uses those decorative stitches to accomplish special techniques, such as quilting or Seminole patchwork. The third discusses the use of tools like machine accessories or needles to create special effects with decorative stitches. The projects included are soft Ultrasuede jewelry, a Christmas card, and Seminole patchwork.

Lesson 37. Decorating with stitches

The simplest, most obvious way to use those flowers, animals and alphabets that are programmed into your machine is to decorate hems and edges. I'm sure everyone with a new machine does that first. But that's only a beginning. Try designing your own fabrics by decorating striped material with rows of programmed stitches. Blue-and-white ticking material looks terrific with red stitches through the white stripes. So simple. And here is an idea using solid-colored fabric with matching thread; stitch evenly spaced rows of stitches over the surface to produce texture. Use this for collars, cuffs, pockets, or self-cov-

ered buttons. An entire jacket might be a life's work.

For the next idea you need a man's striped tie. Choose something that will look smashing with one of your own outfits (look in thrift shops and buy only the widest ones). Open up the tie, remove the lining, press the tie and then back it with tear-away stabilizer. Stitch down the stripes with flowers, stars, triple zigzags, or what-have-you. When you finish, cut out a 1½" or 2" (3.8 or 5cm) wide strip down the length of the tie, depending upon its original width and also on how plump you want the tube to be. Pull off the stabilizer. Fold the strip the long way, with right sides together. Stitch a ¼" (6.3mm) seam and turn to the right side. Stuff the tube with cable cord or thick acrylic yarn and stitch the ends closed, after you have decided its use and what the length must be. I like them with or without a knot in the middle to wear as a neckpiece (sew a snap or Velcro dots at the flattened ends) or tie the tube over wide, Ultrasuede belts.

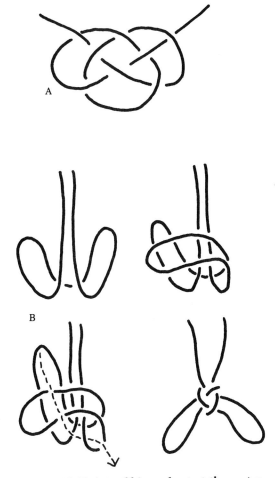

Fig. 11.1A Twist a Chinese knot at the center of the embroidered tube to create a neck-piece. B. Find the center of the tube, then follow the four steps as shown to knot a different soft necklace.

Also twist them into Chinese knots (Fig. 11.1) and frog closures. There are more possibilities when two tubes are knotted together or combined with silky, thick upholstery cord. With the leftovers, I can cover buttons and earrings (but I promise not to wear them all at the same time).

Because a tie is already on the bias, use your embroidered piece as a binding on a purse, vest, or to top a pocket. The following binding method is my favorite way of applying it to an edge. If you want ½" (12.7mm) to show, then multiply that by four (2" or 5cm) and add seam allowances (I use ¼" (6.3mm), which is the measurement from the edge of my presser foot to the center needle position). But you must add two seam allowances—½" or 12.7mm. Your bias strip will be 2½" (6.4cm) wide. Fold the bias wrong sides together and stitch it the long way with a ¼" (6.3mm) seam allowance.

Before you apply the bias to the edge, straight-stitch a guide line ¼" (6.3mm) from the edge you're covering, again using the presser foot as a guide. This takes less time than marking a line with ruler and pen.

Place the binding on the topside of your fabric with the raw edges of the binding on the guideline you've stitched, pin it in place and sew it down, following the stitched line on the bias piece. Next, wrap the bias around the edge to the back. Catch the fold to the stitched line (½" or 12.7mm from the edge) with hand stitches. This binding method creates an even, accurate edge with no raw edges to control on the final, practically invisible, stitching.

I use the same binding method for quilts, but with the binding fabric cut on the straight-of-grain. I do this because using the straight-of-grain ensures me that the edges of my quilts will always remain straight and look neat no matter how many times they are washed or dry-cleaned.

You can use decorative stitches for comforters, too. When it comes time to tie the comforter you're making, embroider one motif where the tie should be instead of using yarn. It's heaven to have a machine that has the capability of starting and stopping on exactly the first and last stitches of a design.

But what if you're not happy with the size of the stitch you've chosen for the comforter—or for any of your decorative projects? On some machines you can change not only the stitch width and length to vary the looks of stitches, but you're also able to elongate or narrow programmed stitches for even greater variety. Check your manual to see if your machine is one of them, then stitch a sample first before you embroider any finished piece. Put the sample in your notebook.

Besides changing the size of stitches, some machines have memories to enable you to combine stitches and even alter some or all of the stitches with functions such as mirror images. This would be a good time to stitch samples of stitches combined with mirror images and balance buttons. Balance buttons enable you to stitch a perfect decoration no matter how bulky or fine your fabric, or you can use them decoratively to change the looks of your stitches: open them up or close them more tightly than their usual appearance. As you can see, a machine with those talents doesn't limit you to the stitches programmed into it. By merely pushing a button or two, you can give a brand new look to a standard stitch.

Here is another way to use rows of decorative stitches: decorate ribbons or bias tape with embroidery. I don't use stabilizer under these. It's too hard to pick out tear-away paper later, and the ribbons or tapes may not take to being dipped in water to remove water-soluble stabilizer. Use a blind hem to shell-stitch edges of bias tape and choose flowers and petals or any open embroidery stitch of your choice to stitch down the center length of either one.

When you do French machine sewing, you can make your own strips of embroidered insertion by choosing a decorative stitch repeat or by combining several in the machine's memory and then stitching yards of 1¼″ (3.15cm) wide strips of the same fabric as your garment. Always cut the strip on the straight of the fabric and then fold the length of it, wrong sides together, pressing lightly to mark the center stitching line. When you finish stitching, you may want to cut the strip narrower before you attach it to entredeaux. Several machines will make entredeaux also. Check your manuals.

If you have an alphabet, use it for greetings on ribbon for packages or on heavy wrapping paper. Program "Happy Birthday" or "Merry Christmas" or stitch the name of the person who will receive your gift. Cover the paper with rows of messages, names or flowers if you have no alphabet. Use open embroidery stitches to keep from cutting too many holes in the paper. If your paper is too fragile, you can back it with tear-away stabilizer, but don't tear it away. And don't limit yourself to red and green papers—use brown Kraft paper or white shelf paper. Your stitching will take it out of the ordinary.

Project
Ultrasuede Pin

Stitching pins to wear on my sweaters or dresses is one way to use up those Ultrasuede scraps that haunt a large box in my sewing room. At the same time, I play with decorative stitches. Ultrasuede is available in bags of scraps by weight, by the inch for belts, and by the yard for garments. I designed a pin to utilize a decorative stitch and found one small silver necklace piece to stitch to it (Fig. 11.2). Look in your drawer of costume jewelry, good jewelry, loose beads and found objects with an eye to someday using one bead, a spacer, the clasp. The next project proves you should never throw anything away.

The blue rectangle can be backed with stabilizer, but it isn't necessary. Use silver metallic thread to embroider rows (the long way) of honeycomb stitches. How do you hide that bottom edge of loose threads? Place the edge ⅜″(9.5mm) from the bottom edge of the green suede (Fig. 11.3B). With topside to topside, stitch across ⅛″ (3.2mm) from the edge of the blue suede. Fold it back and stitch it to the top of the green suede (this will create a soft fold at the bottom of the blue piece and hide your stitches).

Zigzag-stitch the safety pin to the middle of the topside of the red suede. (Look at Ultrasuede closely and you'll see that one side has more nap than the other. The pin is stitched to the napped or topside of the suede because, done this way, more of the napped side will show when the pin is completed.)

Fold the red suede piece ½″ (12.7mm) up from the bottom toward the napped side (back of the pin). Glue it in place. Then place the topside bottom edge of the green suede piece onto the red suede (opposite side from the pin) and align the edges of the red and green pieces. Straight-stitch across the green Ultrasuede to sew it to the red backing, catching both layers of the red suede as you do. Fold up the green and bring it far enough to the top of the red piece to let about ⅛″ (3.2mm) of red fold show beneath it. You'll now have three folds—red, green, and blue. Each one is placed so the one behind it peeks out a bit. Stitch across the top of the blue and green suede again and then fold the top of the red suede over them and zigzag in one place to hold it there (I folded the red down on an angle). Use a bead or found object over the zigzag. My silver piece has a loop at the top and I threaded a long silver cord through it, stitching it through the zigzags by hand so the bead and cord will not shift. Then I

Fig. 11.2 I combined Ultrasuede in three colors, honeycomb stitches, silver cord and one bead to create a soft pin.

143

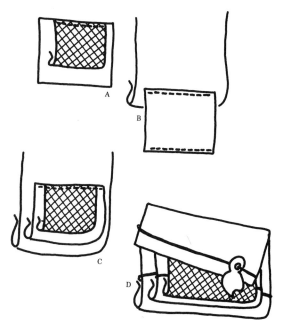

Fig. 11.3 A. Embroider, then attach the piece of blue suede to the green piece. B. Stitch through both layers of red Ultrasuede when attaching the green piece to it. C. Fold up the green suede (blue piece is attached to it) to reveal the fold of red suede beneath. D. Completed pin with silver cord threaded through the bead and wrapped around each layer of fabric.

wrapped the cord around and through the suede pin from both sides—you can see it come out at the sides in Fig. 11.3D (the cord crosses in the middle behind the blue and green pieces). Both ends are brought to the back and glued behind the seam allowance above the red fold.

Project
Christmas Card

Here is another project for built-in stitches (Fig. 11.4). It's a greeting card stitched on paper because I like the unex-

pected and I especially like handmade gifts. If someone makes anything for me, it's special and I keep it forever. I make many gifts, too, and I understand time, thought and energy. Though I think I've tried every art and craft that is known, I always return to my sewing machine. I've block printed, stenciled, and painted Christmas cards, but I stitched this card

Fig. 11.4 This Christmas card is made with wide, striped ribbon held in place with veiling and decorated with embroidery stitches.

Fig. 11.5 Pattern for Christmas card.

145

Stitch width: varies
Stitch length: varies
Needle position: center
Needle: #80
Feed dogs: up
Presser foot: embroidery
Fabric suggestions: 5″ × 7″ (12.7 × 17.8cm) red bridal veil; 5″ (12.7cm) wide red-striped ribbon, 3¼″ (8.3cm) long
Thread: gold metallic
Accessories: 4½″ × 6¾″ (11.4 × 17.1cm) blank greeting card available at craft shops; glue stick

when I found a roll of wide, red-and-white-striped satin ribbon in a box of lace I bought. It is old and fragile, but it works beautifully for the card because it is protected from further disintegration by the veiling. But you don't need ribbon for this project. Use Christmas fabrics or velveteen.

When you choose decorative stitches to use on this card, choose those that are open, rather than a closed satin-stitch type, because you will be cutting into the paper with each stitch. Begin and end on the correct stitch and at the correct place

because every needle hole shows. Always work a sample first and experiment.

First, from the ribbon, cut a triangle for the Christmas tree (Fig. 11.5). The base of the triangle is 3¼″ (8.3cm), the height, 5″ (12.7cm). Use a dot of glue stick to hold it in place on the front of your card. Place the bridal veil over the ribbon to hold down the edges. There's no need to pin or paste, but hold the veiling in place as you stitch. Use an open scallop stitch or another open embroidery stitch of your choice across each stripe. After you've finished the rows of horizontal stitches, choose a stitch to top it—a star? a heart? Stitch it and then cut back the veil into a triangle slightly larger than that of the tree. Add stitches for a trunk and then a border around the edge of the card. If your machine has a star motif, or one similar to it, stitch a scattering of these single designs in the background, but within the border. Leave all thread ends long enough to poke to the back later. (Pull threads to the back, clip them quite short, dab glue on them and press them to the underside of the card.) Back the inside of the card with a piece of white tissue paper cut to size if you want to keep the stitches from showing, and use spray glue or glue stick to hold it in place.

Lesson 38. Sewing techniques using decorative stitches

Many sewing techniques can be taken out of the ordinary by using decorative built-in stitches. The first is quilting. Instead of the usual straight stitch, use a feather stitch-in-the-ditch where you have seamed pieces together, or on whole cloth to make it look pieced. Also, try a serpentine stitch for quilting. There are others equally appropriate, so refer to your manuals.

I use the next idea for wall hangings and banners, but why not for appliqués on clothing? The large size of most hangings necessitates my dividing it into sections, embroidering individual parts of it, then assembling it later. (If I goof up a small piece of fabric I have not ruined the entire wall hanging.) So my appliqué idea for clothing is done the same way. First, draw your design in pencil or water-erasable marker on the appliqué fabric, back it with tear-away stabilizer, and stitch rows of decoration over it to add texture, more color, more interest to a plain appliqué. Start outside the lines of the design. Those stitches will be cut off when you have finished embroidering, and it is not only faster to do it this way—no need to start on exactly the first stitch of a motif—but the edge will look more even. Use one of the methods described in Chapter 4 to apply the appliqué, then satin stitch it to the background fabric.

An idea for those of you who have alphabets and numbers on your machine is to use individual letters and numbers in rows as you would decorative stitches. Many of them are quite decorative when used in repeat patterns. You can also combine them with decorative motifs to create samplers or clever quotes to be framed.

Project
Seminole
Patchwork

This Seminole patchwork technique is specially for those of you who enjoy combining decorative stitches in your machine's memory. Or simplify it by choosing five built-in stitches.

Stitch width: 0 to widest
Stitch length: varies
Decorative stitch: combine stitches in memory; or use 5 different built-in stitches
Presser foot: embroidery
Fabric suggestions: four different solid-colored fabrics, three strips 2″ (5.0cm) × 18″ (45.7cm), one strip 5″ (12.7cm) × 18″ (45.7cm)
Thread: machine-embroidery

Cut out three different-colored strips of fabric, each on at least 2″ (5.0cm) wide and 18″ (45.7cm) long. Mark the center of one by folding the strip in half the long way, pressing and then marking, with a water-erasable marker, ¼″ seam allowances on each edge. Between the center and the seam allowance markings on this piece, draw two evenly spaced stitching lines on *each* side of the fold. Use adding machine tape as a stabilizer and sew five straight lines of decorative stitches (on the center fold and the two lines drawn on either

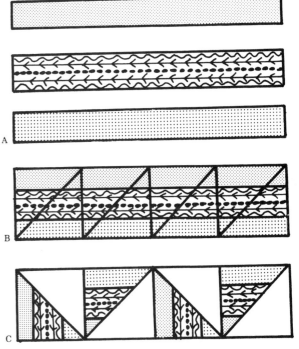

Fig. 11.6 Making a strip of Seminole patchwork. A. Decorate one strip of fabric with rows of built-in stitches and combine it with two other strips of plain fabric. B. Sew the pieces together, then cut into triangles as shown. C. Cut a fourth strip of fabric, as wide as the combined strips in B, cut the strip into triangles as you did in B. First stitch the triangles into squares, then into a long strip.

side). When that is completed, stitch one strip of plain fabric to each side of the decorated strip, right sides together, using a ¼″ (6.3mm) seam allowance (Fig. 11.6B). Cut out a fourth strip of fabric in a fourth color, the same size as the colorful strip you have stitched together. Cut both strips into triangles, combine them into squares, and then combine the squares into a strip (Fig. 11.6C).

Lesson 39.Using machine accessories with decorative stitches

Sometimes decorative stitches can be used along with sewing machine accessories to produce exciting results. Use the circle maker and different programmed stitches to embellish fabric with decorative circles. Place your fabric in a hoop for this technique. Overlap some of the circles and stitch circles in different sizes, but remember to do samples first. When stitching circles, decorative stitches don't always end at the exact spot you want them to, so upon nearing the completion of the circle, sew slowly. You may have to push or pull back carefully on your fabric, or stop and move it, to make the join pleasing.

Another accessory to use with decorative stitches is the bias binder attachment. Be sure you have the zigzag model and then apply lace or bias tapes to fabric, using an interesting stitch.

Don't ignore hemstitching or double needles when using bult-in stitches; but before you start, be sure the needles clear the opening in the needleplate on their farthest swing. With double needles, stitch over cords on top or use one cord threaded through the throat plate. Experiment. Choose a stitch that will cover, then uncover, the cord (or cords) as it's completed. Depending upon your choices of cord, thread and cord colors, there are many decorative possibilities to be achieved.

CHAPTER 12

Making the Tote Bag

The year I became program chairman for an embroiderer's guild, I began to assess previous programs: Why was one a success, another a failure? I remembered the many needlework workshops I had taken, the many projects I had started in those classes and never finished because they were too big or demanded too much of my time. And I knew I wasn't the only one who felt this way, as other members also had boxes of half-finished needlework.

That's when I came up with the idea of the tote bag. I asked the teachers that year to gear their workshops toward making samples small enough to fit in a 6" (15.2cm) square frame. The fabric squares could then fit into the frames made by the handles on a tote bag I designed. Each new square could easily slip in and out. Not only were the class projects small enough to complete easily, but they were useful and decorative as well.

I'm using the same tote bag for this book (Fig. 12.1). After you've made the tote bag, it can be used to show off the sample squares found in the lessons.

First, I'll explain how to finish the squares you made throughout the lessons in this book. Then I'll explain the tote bag.

Finishing the squares

Specific instructions for each square are included in the lessons. A brief recap: Start with a piece of fabric large enough to fit in a 7" (17.8cm) hoop, if you will be working with one. I suggest starting with a 9"

(22.9cm) square, as it is better to have extra fabric than not enough. The finished square will be 6¾" (17.1cm). The area that will show in the frame will be 6" (15.2cm) square. Cut a piece of acetate or cardboard 6¾" (17.1cm) square to use as a template.

After completing the embroidery, quilting, appliqué—whatever the lesson calls

Fig. 12.1 The tote bag, with one of the squares in position on the pocket.

for–center the acetate pattern over the square. Draw a line at the edge of the acetate all the way around with a water-erasable marker or white chalk pencil.

Back the square with stiff fabric, fleece, or iron-on interfacing if it is not stiff enough for the pocket. Stitch along the line you've drawn and cut off the extra fabric to that line.

Slip typing paper or heavy tear-away stabilizer under the square. Finish by satin stitching at stitch width 4 around the edge. Dab the corners with Fray-Check to keep them from raveling.

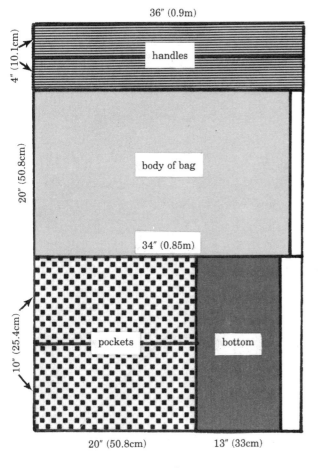

Fig. 12.2 Layout for the tote bag.

Glue or stitch Velcro dots under the corner of each square to correspond to the ones in the pocket frame. (If the square is stiff enough, this will not be necessary.) An alternative to Velcro is an idea from Marilyn Tisol of Hinsdale, Illinois. She backs each square she makes by first cutting a piece of plastic canvas the size of the square; then she attaches the fabric square to it by whipping the edges together. The plastic is rigid enough to keep the square in the frame.

Tote bag construction

My tote bag is made of canvas, but it can be made of any heavy-duty fabric. I used canvas because I wanted a bag that would stand by itself. If the fabric you've chosen is not heavy enough, press a layer of fusible webbing between two layers of material. Whatever you choose, pre-wash and press all fabrics before you cut.

Supplies:
1½ yards (1.4m) of 36″ (0.9m) canvas (includes body of bag, handles, pockets, and bottom of bag)
3⅛ yards (3m) of 1″ (2.5cm) wide fusible webbing
Teflon pressing sheet
Four Velcro dots
Sewing thread to match canvas, or monofilament
Rotary cutter and board are timesavers
24″ × 6″ (60.9 × 15.2cm) plastic ruler
Water-erasable pen, pencil or sliver of soap
Edging foot, zigzag or jeans foot
Jeans needle

My tote (see color insert) is made up of many colors and looks as if Dr. Seuss invented it. It includes royal blue for the bottom, yellow pockets, green handles, and red for the body of the bag.

I chose those colors because the striped lining fabric included them all. I backed the lining with Pellon fleece and quilted

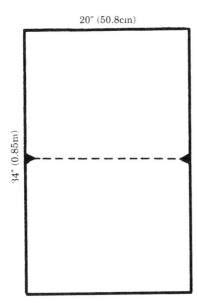

20″ (50.8cm)

34″ (0.85m)

Fig. 12.3 Notch and mark the inside of the bag.

down each stripe to give my bag even more body. I added pockets to the lining, too.

Lining is optional, but if you choose to include one, you will need another piece of fabric at least 34″ × 20″ (86.4cm × 50.8cm). Add 20″ × 20″ (50.8cm × 50.8cm) to this if you wish to make pockets for your lining.

The layout of the bag is provided in Fig. 12.2; note that the layout is predicated on cutting all pieces from a single length of cloth, rather than several different colors.

Body of bag:
34″ × 20″ (0.85m × 50.8cm)

1. Cut out fabric. Fold in half and notch bottom on both sides, 17″ (43.2cm) from top. Draw a line between the notches on the inside (Fig. 12.3).

2. Place a 1″ (2.5cm) strip of fusible webbing along both 20″ (50.8cm) edges on the right side of the bag and fuse in place using the Teflon pressing sheet. Fold at the top of the webbing to the backside. Press the

fold, using the Teflon pressing sheet on top to protect your iron. Then fold over 1″ (2.5cm) again, using the pressing sheet *between* the fusible webbing and the body of the bag.

3. Mark a line down the length of this piece 6¼″ (15.8cm) from each side, as shown in Fig. 12.4 to use later as guidelines for construction of the bag.

Pockets: 10″ × 20″
(25.4cm × 50.8cm); cut 2

1. Use the ruler and marking pen to indicate stitching lines from top to bottom—6¼″ (15.8cm) from each side. Center area will be 7½″ (19.1cm).

2. Cut slits 1½″ (3.8cm) down from the top on these lines. Make a mark ¾″ (19.0mm) from the top and another ¾″ (19.0mm) down from the first. Draw lines through those marks across the top of the pockets (Fig. 12.5A). It is easier if you mark the middle section on the *back* of the

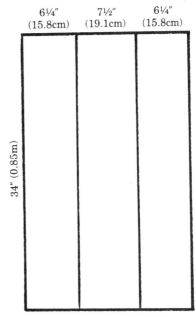

6¼″ (15.8cm)	7½″ (19.1cm)	6¼″ (15.8cm)

34″ (0.85m)

Fig. 12.4 Mark the outside of the bag.

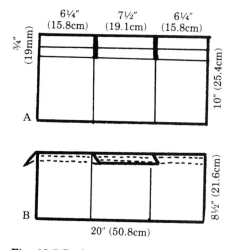

Fig. 12.5 Pocket construction. A. Mark lines to indicate the pockets. Then mark lines across the pockets, ¾" (19.0mm) and 1½" (3.8cm) from the top. Cut down 1½" (3.8cm) between the pockets. B. Fold the tops of the side pockets to the back, the top of the middle pocket to the front.

frames in which you'll slip the 6" (15.2mm) squares.

Handles: 4" × 36" (10.2cm × 0.9m); cut 2

1. Stitch down one long side 1" (2.5cm) from edge. Fold. Do the same with the other side. (This stitching is used as a guide to make folding the handles easier and more accurate.) Bring folded edges together and fold again, creating the 1" (2.5cm) wide handles. Place strips of 1" (2.5cm) fusible webbing inside the length of the handles and press to fuse. The handle is four layers (plus fusible webbing) thick (Fig. 12.6).

2. Topstitch both sides ⅛" (3.2mm) from edge. Use the edging foot with needle posi-

fabric, so you'll be able to see the lines as you fold. Fold on the lines as follows: Each side should be folded twice toward the inside of the bag. The middle 7½" (19.1cm) should be folded twice toward the front of the fabric. This middle flap creates the top of the frame.

3. Stitch across the top of all three pockets ⅛" (3.2mm) from the top edge. Do this on both pocket pieces.

4. Then stitch across side pocket sections through all three layers of fabric at ⅛" (3.2mm) from each bottom fold. Finish both side pockets on both pocket pieces this way (Fig. 12.5B).

5. Open out the top of the middle sections on both pocket pieces to enable you to stitch across the folds without stitching them to the pockets. Stitch across the 7½" (19.1cm) middle sections on both pocket pieces at ⅛" (3.2mm) from each bottom fold. This flap will create the top of the

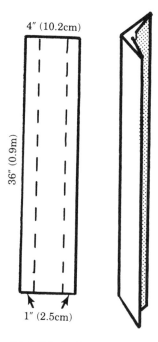

Fig. 12.6 Stitch down the length of the handles 1" (2.5cm) from each side. Fold down 1" (2.5cm) at each side, the length of the handle. Then fold the handle in half. Place strip of fusible webbing inside and press in place. Stitch the handles together.

tion at far left. Then sew ¼″ (6.3mm) in from those lines of stitches on both sides.

Bottom: 13″ × 20″
(33cm × 50.8cm)

1. Fold over 1″ (2.5cm) top and bottom along the 20″ (50.8cm) edges and topstitch across ⅛″ (3.2mm) from the fold. Draw a line ¾″ (19.0mm) from each fold.

2. Fold the bottom in half the long way and notch on the fold on both sides, 6½″ (16.5cm) from top and bottom (Fig. 12.7).

Assembly

1. First sew pockets to the bag. The pockets will be 3″ (7.5cm) from the top. (Remember that the bag has been folded over 2″ (5.1cm) at the top. Measure from the top of the last fold. Line up the markings, 6¼″ (15.9cm) from each side on bag and pockets and pin in place. Stitch on the lines you've drawn to create pockets and, using a ¼″ (6.3mm) seam allowance, stitch down each side and across the bottoms of the pocket pieces.

2. Sew handles next. Find the center of the bag by folding it double the long way. Measure 3″ (7.6cm) from the center to each side of the bag and make a mark with the water-erasable pen; 6″ (15.2cm) will be open in center. Using the 24″ × 6″ (60.9cm × 15.2cm) ruler, draw guidelines through these marks the length of the bag. Pin handles in place outside those lines. Stitch across the bottom of the handles and up, ⅛″ (3.2mm) from the edge, on the existing outside stitching. Extend your stitching all the way to the top of the bag. Do this on the next outside lines as well (you will often stitch on top of other lines of stitching). The top edge of the bag will not be sewn down until later, but sew through the folds as you attach the handles.

3. To make the open frame, stitch only the top of the handles above the pockets on both sides. Leave ¾″ (19.0mm) around the frame to insert workshop squares (Fig. 12.8).

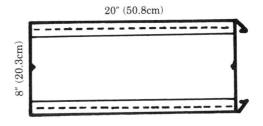

20″ (50.8cm)

8″ (20.3cm)

Fig. 12.7 Follow this diagram to fold, mark and stitch the bottom piece of the bag.

4. Attach bottom next. Match notches with those of the bag and pin the bottom in place. Stitch over the ⅛″ (3.2mm) stitching line to ¾″ (19.0mm) from each side of the center pocket (see Fig. 12.8). *Do not* stitch across the center pocket. Then stitch all across the bottom piece on the ¾″ (19.0mm) mark. This will create the bottom of the frame. Double check. Is the frame done correctly? Be sure you can slip a fabric square inside.

5. Finish the side edges of the bag with a zigzag stitch (Fig. 12.9). Then put it all together. Fold at center bottom notches with right sides together. Check to see that pockets and bottom meet at each side. Stitch in a ⅝″ (15.9mm) seam line from top to bottom. Now refold the top edge of the bag and press in place to fuse. Topstitch in place at the top edge and bottom fold.

6. Bag corners should be finished this way: On the inside, pinch the bottom by matching the side seam with the line drawn across the inside of the bottom of the bag (Fig. 12.10). Measure, on the seam line, 2″ (5.1cm) from the point. Draw a line across. Be sure it is exact on each side so stitching is perpendicular to the side seams. Stitch on drawn line for corners. This forms the bottom of the bag. If you wish to cut a piece of ⅛″ (3.2mm) Masonite or linoleum tile to fit the bottom, do so now before you line your bag.

7. Press one side of four adhesive-backed

153

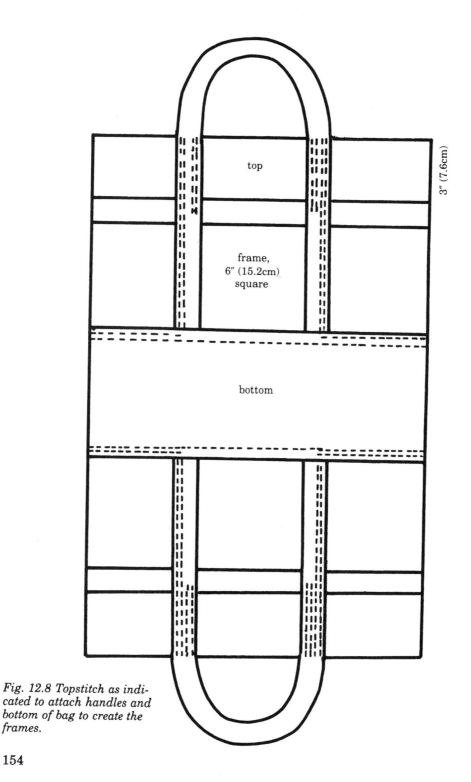

top

frame,
6″ (15.2cm)
square

3″ (7.6cm)

bottom

Fig. 12.8 Topstitch as indi-
cated to attach handles and
bottom of bag to create the
frames.

Fig. 12.9 Finish the edges with zigzag stitches. With right sides together, stitch each side of the tote bag.

Fig. 12.10 Make the tote bag corners by stitching lines perpendicular to the side seams, 2″ (5.1cm) up from the points.

Velcro dots into the four corners of the frame.

Lining

If you line your bag, create the lining as if making another bag. Do not include bottom, pockets or handles. However, if you wish to add pockets to the lining, then cut out two pieces of 10″ × 20″ (25.4cm × 50.8cm) fabric, the same size as the bag pockets. At the top of each pocket piece, turn over 1″ (2.5cm) two times and sew down at the top and at the fold. Press up 1″ (2.5cm) at the bottom. Place the pocket pieces 3″ (7.6cm) from the top of the lining and pin in place. Sew across the bottom of the pocket at the fold and ¾″ (19.0mm) from the first stitching line. (The double line of stitching will add strength to the pockets.) Then attach the pockets to the sides of the lining by stitching down on each side with a ¼″ (6.3mm) seam allowance. With a ruler and water-erasable marker, draw lines down the pocket pieces to indicate where you will divide the fabric for pockets. Stitch those in place.

Sew up the sides of the lining, using a ⅝″ (15.9mm) seam allowance) and create the bottom corner. Fold over the top as you did for the bag. I use the double fold for stability.

Whip stitch invisibly by hand around the top to keep the lining and bag together. With heavy canvas, you may prefer to make the lining and then place wrong sides together (bag and lining) and machine stitch around the top.

AFTERWORD

Know Your Sewing Machine could go on forever, as there is no way to include, in one book, everything that can be accomplished by your machine.

I hope you're inspired to experiment, to fill your notebook with samples, and to take those long-cuts, choosing decorative over mundane.

A Short History
of the Sewing Machine

by ROBBIE FANNING

No single inventor can be credited with the invention of the sewing machine, because over a 60-year period many people contributed pieces of the puzzle. The problem? Inventors needed to make a paradigm shift, a change in their thinking, in order to devise a machine.

Put yourself in their boots: if you were trying to invent a machine to simulate hand sewing, wouldn't you start by mounting a hand-sewing needle in some sort of device? Now think about the location of the eye in a hand-sewing vs. a sewing-machine needle. Eureka—paradigm shift! The change in thinking occurred when Elias Howe moved the eye to the pointed end of the needle. (Reputedly, his wife dreamed about savages chasing them with giant sewing-machine needles, which became the impetus for invention.)

The other paradigm shift was to use two threads, one above the fabric and one below, to form a lockstitch, rather than to use one thread, as in handsewing. This invention is credited to Walter Hunt in the 1830s.

The early reception to the sewing machine was skepticism. When Barthelemy Timmonier invented a machine in 1841 to mass-produce uniforms for the French Army, local tailors rioted in protest and destroyed all the machines.

Even I. M. Singer was skeptical at first. As reported in Ruth Brandon's *A Capitalist Romance: Singer and the Sewing Machine*, "When first approached to abandon his type-carving machine and work on inventing a better sewing machine, Singer said 'What a devilish machine! You want to do away with the only thing that keeps women quiet, their sewing!' "

Women were scared by the new machine. To allay their suspicions, Singer set up lavish showrooms with carpeting, carved wooden furniture, and ornate decorations. Attractive young saleswomen demonstrated the machines, in an effort to make them not only respectable to proper Victorian women—but also approachable.

It didn't take long for customers to recognize the labor-saving potential of the new machine. The sewing machine quickly became the first consumer appliance to have wide distribution. Buying a machine in 1858 prodded the same neighborly curiosity as having the first TV on the block in 1950. By 1900, most every household had a sewing machine, just as today 98% of us own a TV.

Most major changes on the machine were made between 1900 and 1945: the zigzag machine, the addition of electricity, the ability to sew backward and forward, the reverse cycle stitches that allow precise decorative stitches to be formed. But today we are in the midst of dramatic changes, accomplished by the marriage of the microchip and the sewing machine. Today all the major brands sell computerized machines, each season bringing exciting refinements like the ability to program your own stitches. Who knows what tomorrow's machine will do?

Further resources:

Brandon, Ruth, *A Capitalist Romance; Singer and the Sewing Machine*, JB Lippincott Co., 1977.

Cooper, Grace Rogers, *The Sewing Machine/Its Invention and Development*, Smithsonian Institution Press, 1976.

Major events in the history of the sewing machine

1790: Thomas Saint patents a forerunner of the chain-stitch machine in England.

1830: Barthelemy Timmonier, a French tailor, patents a simple chain-stitch machine.

1841: Fearing unemployment, angry tailors destroy 80 Timmonier machines bought by the French Army for uniforms.

1832–34: Walter Hunt, United States, constructs a two-thread machine with an oscillating shuttle, making possible the lockstitch. He never patents the invention.

1846: Without ever hearing of Hunt's invention, Elias Howe, U.S., constructs a lockstitch machine with an eye-pointed needle. The invention is sold to an English corset manufacturer. A flurry of interest and refinements— e.g., adequate feed mechanisms, a horizontal support for the cloth—occurs in England and the U.S.

1851: Isaac Merritt Singer, U.S., patents a machine so similar to Howe's that the latter sues.

1856: Four manufacturers form the "Sewing Machine Combination" and agree to pool patents and to pay Howe royalties.

1860: 111,000 sewing machines are manufactured by 74 U.S. companies, up from 0 manufactured in 1850.

1889: Singer introduces the first electric sewing machine for home use, but it isn't popular until the 1920s.

1900: First zigzag machine is used in industry to sew window blinds.

1905: The electric sewing machine is important to industry by this date.

1911: *Singer Instructions for Art Embroidery*, a treasury of machine-embroidery techniques, is published.

1921: Singer introduces the first truly portable electric home sewing machine.

1931: Singer adds backward sewing and exact stitch length control.

1945: The home zigzag machine becomes popular after World War II, which had prevented the import of European-made machines.

1980: Viking introduces the first computerized sewing machine with an alphabet and calls it "The Writing Machine."

Sources of Supply

Sewing Machine Companies

Archer-Finesse
Melex USA Inc.
1200 Front St.
Raleigh, NC 27609

Bernina of America
534 W. Chestnut
Hinsdale, IL 60521

Brother Sewing Machine Co.
8th Corporation Pl.
Piscataway, NJ 08854

Elna Inc.
7642 Washington Ave. S
Minneapolis, MN 55344

Kenmore
Sears Tower
Chicago, IL 60607

Necchi Logica/Allyn International
1075 Santa Fe Dr.
Denver, CO 80203

Nelco
164 W. 25th St.
New York, NY 10001

New Home Sewing Machine Co.
171 Commerce Dr.
Carlstadt, NJ 07072

J.C. Penney Co., Inc.
1301 Avenue of the Americas
New York, NY 10019

Pfaff American Sales Corp.
610 Winters Ave.
Paramus, NJ 07653

Riccar America Co.
14281 Franklin Ave.
Tustin, CA 92680

Simplicity/Tacony Corp.
4421 Ridgewood Ave.
St. Louis, MO 63116

Singer Co.
135 Raritan Center Pkwy.
Edison, NJ 08837

Viking White Sewing Machine Co.
11750 Berea Rd.
Cleveland, OH 44111

Ward's (Montgomery Ward)
PO Box 8339
Chicago, IL 60680

(**Note**: The following listings were adapted with permission from *The Complete Book of Machine Embroidery* by Robbie and Tony Fanning [Chilton, 1986].)

Threads

Note: Ask your local retailer or send a pre-addressed stamped envelope to the companies below to find out where to buy their threads.

Extra-fine

Assorted threads
Robison-Anton Textile Co.
175 Bergen Blvd.
Fairview, NJ 07022

DMC 100% cotton, Sizes 30 and 50
The DMC Corporation
107 Trumbull Street
Elizabeth, NJ 07206

Dual-Duty Plus Extra-fine, cotton-wrapped polyester
J&PCoats/Coats & Clark
PO Box 6044
Norwalk, CT 06852

Iris 100% rayon
Art Sales
4801 W. Jefferson
Los Angeles, CA 90016

Iris 100% silk—*see* Zwicky

Madeira threads
Madeira Co.
56 Primrose Drive
O'Shea Industrial Park
Laconia, NH 03246

Mettler Metrosene Fine Machine Embroidery
cotton, Size 60/2
> Swiss-Metrosene, Inc.
> 7780 Quincy Street
> Willowbrook, IL 60521

Natesh 100% rayon, lightweight
> Aardvark Adventures
> PO Box 2449
> Livermore, CA 94550

Paradise 100% rayon
> D&E Distributing
> 199 N. El Camino Real #F-242
> Encinitas, CA 92024

Sulky 100% rayon, Sizes 30 and 40
> Speed Stitch, Inc.
> PO Box 3472
> Port Charlotte, FL 33949

Zwicky 100% cotton, Size 30/2
> White Sewing Machine Co.
> 11750 Berea Rd.
> Cleveland, OH 44111

Ordinary

Dual Duty Plus, cotton-wrapped polyester—
see Dual Duty Plus Extra-fine

Also Natesh heavyweight, Zwicky in cotton
and polyester, Mettler Metrosene in 30/2, 40/
3, 50/3, and 30/3, and Metrosene Plus

Metallic

> YLI Corporation
> 45 West 300 North
> Provo, UT 84601

> Troy Thread & Textile Corp.
> 2300 W. Diversey Ave.
> Chicago, IL 60647
> > Free catalog

Machine-Embroidery Supplies

(hoops, threads, patterns, books, etc.)

> Aardvark Adventures
> PO Box 2449
> Livermore, CA 94550
> > Also publishes "Aardvark Territorial
> > Enterprise"

> Clotilde Inc.
> 237 SW 28th St.
> Ft. Lauderdale, FL 33315

Craft Gallery Ltd.
PO Box 8319
Salem, MA 01971

D&E Distributing
199 N. El Camino Real #F-242
Encinitas, CA 92024

Verna Holt's Machine Stitchery
PO Box 236
Hurricane, UT 84734

Nancy's Notions
PO Box 683
Beaver Dam, WI 53916
> Catalog $.60 in stamps

Patty Lou Creations
Rt 2, Box 90-A
Elgin, OR 97827

Sew-Art International
PO Box 550
Bountiful, UT 84010
> Catalog $2

Speed Stitch, Inc.
PO Box 3472
Port Charlotte, FL 33952
> Catalog $2

SewCraft
Box 1869
Warsaw, IN 46580
> Also publishes newsletter/catalog

Treadleart
25834 Narbonne Ave.
Lomita, CA 90717

Sewing Machine Supplies

The Button Shop
PO Box 1065
Oak Park, IL 60304
> Presser feet

Sewing Emporium
1087 Third Avenue
Chula Vista, CA 92010
> Presser feet, accessories

Miscellaneous

Applications
871 Fourth Ave.
Sacramento, CA 95818
> Release Paper for appliqué

Berman Leathercraft
145 South St.
Boston, MA 02111
    Leather

Boycan's Craft and Art Supplies
PO Box 897
Sharon, PA 16146
    Plastic needlepoint canvas

Cabin Fever Calicoes
PO Box 54
Center Sandwich, NH 03227

Clearbrook Woolen Shop
PO Box 8
Clearbrook, VA 22624
    Ultrasuede scraps

The Fabric Carr
170 State St.
Los Altos, CA 94022
    Sewing gadgets

Folkwear
Box 3798
San Rafael, CA 94912
    Timeless fashion patterns – $1 catalog

The Green Pepper Inc.
941 Olive Street
Eugene, OR 97401
    Outdoor fabrics, patterns – $1 catalog

Home-Sew
Bethlehem, PA 18018
    Lace – $.25 catalog

Libby's Creations
PO Box 16800 Ste. 180
Mesa, AZ 85202
    Horizontal spool holder

LJ Originals, Inc.
516 Sumac Pl.
DeSoto, TX 75115
    TransGraph

Lore Lingerie
3745 Overland Ave.
Los Angeles, CA 90034
    1 lb. of silk remnants, $9.45

Osage Country Quilt Factory
400 Walnut
Overbrook, KS 66524
    Washable fabric spray glue

The Pellon Company
119 West 40th St.
New York, NY 10018
    Machine appliqué supplies

The Perfect Notion
115 Maple St.
Toms River, NJ 08753
    Sewing supplies

Salem Industries, Inc.
PO Box 43027
Atlanta, GA 30336
    Olfa cutters, rulers

Solar-Kist Corp.
PO Box 273
LaGrange, IL 60525
    Teflon pressing sheet

Stacy Industries, Inc.
38 Passaic St.
Wood-Ridge, NJ 07075
    Teflon pressing sheet

Summa Design
Box 24404
Dayton, OH 45424
    Charted designs for knitting needle machine sewing

Susan of Newport
Box 3107
Newport Beach, CA 92663
    Ribbons and laces

Tandy Leather Co.
PO Box 791
Ft. Worth, TX 76101
    Leather

Theta's School of Sewing
2508 N.W. 39th Street
Oklahoma City, OK 73112
    Charted designs for knitting needle machine sewing, smocking directions and supplies for the machine

Magazines
(write for rates)

Aardvark Territorial Enterprise
PO Box 2449
Livermore, CA 94550
    Newspaper jammed with all kinds of information about all kinds of embroidery, design, and things to order. I ordered the gold rings from them.

disPatch
1042 E. Baseline
Tempe, AZ 85283
    Newspaper about quilting and machine arts

Fiberarts
50 College St.
Asheville, NC 28801
    Gallery of the best fiber artists, including those who work in machine stitchery.

Needlecraft for Today
4949 Byers
Ft. Worth, TX 76109
    Creative uses of the sewing machine

SewCraft
Box 1869
Warsaw, IN 46580
    Newspaper and catalog combination containing machine embroidery articles, designs and supplies.

Sew News
PO Box 1790
Peoria, IL 61656
    Monthly tabloid, mostly about garment sewing

Threads
Box 355
Newton, CT 06470
    Magazine on all fiber crafts

Treadleart
25834 Narbonne Ave., Ste. 1
Lomita, CA 90717
    Bimonthly about machine embroidery

Bibliography

Alexander, Eugenie, *Fabric Pictures*, Mills and Boon Ltd., London, 1967.

Ashley, Clifford W., *The Ashley Book of Knots*, Doubleday & Co., 1944.

Bennet, dj, *Machine Embroidery with Style*, Madrona Publishers, 1980.

Butler, Anne, *Machine Stitches*, BT Batsford, Ltd., 1976.

Clucas, Joy, *Your Machine for Embroidery*, G. Bell & Sons, 1975.

Coleman, Anne, *The Creative Sewing Machine*, BT Batsford, 1979.

Ericson, Lois, *Fabrics. . .Reconstructed* (Lois Ericson, Box 1680, Tahoe City, CA 95730), 1985.

———, *Belts. . .Waisted Sculpture*, 1984.

Fanning, Robbie and Tony, *The Complete Book of Machine Quilting*, Chilton Book Co., 1980.

———, *The Complete Book of Machine Embroidery*, Chilton Book Co., 1986.

Gray, Jennifer, *Machine Embroidery*, Van Nostrand Reinhold, 1973.

Hall, Carolyn, *The Sewing Machine Craft Book*, Van Nostrand Reinhold, 1980.

Harding, Valerie, *Textures in Embroidery*, Watson-Guptill, New York, 1977.

Hazen, Gale Grigg, *Sew Sane* (The Sewing Place, 100 W. Rincon Ave., Ste. 105, Campbell, CA 95008; $14.95 postpaid), 1985.

Hogue, Refa D., *Machine Edgings* (c/o Treadleart, 25834 Narbonne Avenue, Lomita, CA 90717).

Hoover, Doris and Nancy Welch, *Tassels* (out-of-print), 1978.

James, Irene, *Sewing Specialties*, I. M. James Enterprises, 1982.

Lawrence and Clotilde, *Sew Smart*, IBC Publishing Co., 1984.

———, Supplement, IBC Publishing Co., 1984.

Macor, Alida, *And Sew On*, Alida Macor, 1985.

McNeill, Moyra, *Machine Embroidery—Lace and See-Through Techniques*, BT Batsford, 1985.

Nall, Mary Lou, *Mary Lou's Sewing Tchniques* (c/o Treadleart, 25834 Narbonne Avenue, Lomita, CA 90717).

Nicholas, Annwen, *Embroidery in Fashion*, Watson-Guptill, 1975.

Ota, Kimi, *Sashiko Quilting* (Kimi Ota, 10300 61st Ave. So., Seattle, Washington 98178), 1981.

Pullen, Martha, *French Hand Sewing by Machine* (518 Madison St., Huntsville, AL 35801), 1985.

Shaeffer, Claire B., *The Complete Book of Sewing Short Cuts*, Sterling Publishing Co., Inc., 1984.

Short, Eirian, *Quilting*, BT Batsford, London, 1983.

Skjerseth, Douglas Neil, *Stitchology*, Seth Publications (PO Box 1606, Novato, CA 94947), 1979.

Thompson, Sue, *Decorative Dressmaking*, Rodale Press, 1985.

Warren, Virena, *Landscape in Embroidery*, BT Batsford, 1986.

Wiechec, Philomena, *Celtic Quilt Designs*, Celtic Design Co., 1980.

Zieman, Nancy, *The Busy Woman's Sewing Book*, Nancy's Notions Ltd., 1984.

Index